PERT MATH TEST SUCCESS

ADVANTAGE+ EDITION

PERT Math Study Guide and Practice Tests

PERT Math Test Success Advantage Plus Edition: PERT Math Study Guide and Practice Tests

ISBN: 978-1-949282-53-5

Note: PERT and the Postsecondary Educational Readiness Test are trademarks of McCann Testing. Neither McCann Testing nor the Florida Department of Education are affiliated with or endorse this publication.

PERT Test Information

The Florida PERT (Postsecondary Educational Readiness Test) is a placement test that your college will administer in order to assess your mathematical, reading, and writing skills. The PERT is an untimed computer-adaptive test. This means that you will take the test on a computer and that your response to previous questions will determine the difficulty level of subsequent questions. In other words, if you are answering the questions correctly, the problems should become more difficult as the test progresses.

Test questions on the PERT are multiple-choice. Since the PERT is a secure test, the items in this book are not actual test questions. However, this practice material is designed to review the necessary mathematical skills covered on the PERT Exam by simulating the difficulty level and format of questions you may face on the actual test.

While you cannot pass or fail the PERT, your results from the exam will be used to place you into classes during your freshman year. If you perform poorly on the exam, you may need to take non-credit developmental classes that will cost you both time and money. It is therefore worthwhile to be well prepared for the examination.

How to Use this Publication

You should study the tips and example problems in the math concept and formula review in Part 1 of the book first.

While going through the study guide in Part 1, you should pay special attention to the exam tips, which are highlighted in the "A+" boxes.

When you have studied the tips and sample problems, you should then proceed to the practice tests in Part 2 of the book.

Please be sure to complete all three of the PERT math practice tests in this publication as each practice test increases in level of difficulty.

Then complete the 100 bonus exercises in the last section of the study guide and check your answers.

TABLE OF CONTENTS

PART 1 – STUDY GUIDE WITH MATH CONCEPT AND FORMULA REVIEW

Applying Standard Concepts:

Although the PERT test will usually will not have questions covering standard concepts, students will be required to understand standard concepts in order to solve more complex problems on the exam. Students should therefore have a good understanding of the following basic mathematical skills:

- Computations with Integers

- Basic Operations with Fractions

- Basic Operations with Mixed Numbers

- Order of Operations

- Percentages and Decimals

- Proportions

- Ratios

- Setting Up Basic Equations

- Working with Averages

Please study the sample problems in this section if you need to refresh your skills in any of the above areas.

Computations with Integers

Computations with integers are assessed on the PERT examination.

Integers are positive and negative whole numbers. Integers cannot have decimals, nor can they be mixed numbers. In other words, they can't contain fractions.

One of the most important concepts to remember about integers is that two negative signs together make a positive number.

Why do two negatives make a positive? In plain English, you can think of it like using "not" two times in one sentence.

For example, you tell your friend: "I do not want you to not go to the party."

In the sentence above, you are really telling your friend that you want him or her to attend the party.

In other words, the "two negatives" concept in math is similar to the "two negatives" concept in the English language.

So, when you see a number like $-(-2)$ you have to use 2 in your calculation.

Look at the example problem that follows.

Problem 1:

$-(-5) + 3 = ?$

A.   −8

B.   −2

C.   2

D.   8

The correct answer is D.

According to the concepts stated above, we know that $-(-5) = 5$

So, we can substitute this into the equation in order to solve it.

$-(-5) + 3 = ?$

$5 + 3 = 8$

You will also see problems that ask you to perform multiplication or division on integers.

Some of these problems may ask you to find an integer that meets certain mathematical requirements, like in problem 2 below.

Problem 2:

What is the largest possible product of two even integers whose sum is 22?

A. 11

B. 44

C. 100

D. 120

The correct answer is D.

For problems that ask you to find the largest possible product of two even integers, first you need to divide the sum by 2.

The sum in this problem is 22, so we need to divide this by 2.

$22 \div 2 = 11$

Now take the result from this division and find the 2 nearest even integers that are 1 number higher and lower.

$11 + 1 = 12$

$11 - 1 = 10$

Then multiply these two numbers together in order to get the product.

$12 \times 10 = 120$

Fractions – Multiplying

You will see problems on the exam that ask you to multiply fractions.

When multiplying fractions, multiply the numerators from each fraction. Then multiply the denominators.

The numerator is the number on the top of each fraction.

The denominator is the number on the bottom of the fraction.

Problem:

What is $^1/_3 \times {}^2/_3$?

A. $^2/_3$

B. $^2/_6$

C. $^2/_9$

D. $^1/_3$

The correct answer is C.

Multiply the numerators.

$1 \times 2 = 2$

Then multiply the denominators.

$3 \times 3 = 9$

These numbers form the new fraction.

$^2/_9$

Fractions – Dividing

You will also need to know how to divide fractions for the exam.

To divide fractions, invert the second fraction by putting the denominator on the top and numerator on the bottom. Then multiply.

Problem:

$$\frac{1}{5} \div \frac{4}{7} = ?$$

A. $\frac{4}{20}$

B. $\frac{7}{20}$

C. $\frac{4}{35}$

D. $\frac{5}{35}$

The correct answer is B.

Remember to invert the second fraction by putting the denominator on the top and the numerator on the bottom.

Our problem was: $\frac{1}{5} \div \frac{4}{7} = ?$

So the second fraction $\frac{4}{7}$ becomes $\frac{7}{4}$ when inverted.

Now use the inverted fraction to solve the problem.

$$\frac{1}{5} \div \frac{4}{7} =$$

$$\frac{1}{5} \times \frac{7}{4} = \frac{7}{20}$$

Fractions – Finding the Lowest Common Denominator (LCD)

In some fraction problems, you will have to find the lowest common denominator.

In other words, before you add or subtract fractions, you have to change them so that the bottom numbers in each fraction are the same.

You do this by multiplying the numerator [top number] by the same number you use on the denominator for each fraction.

A+ Remember to multiply the numerator and denominator by the same number when you are converting to the LCD.

Problem:

What is $\dfrac{1}{9} + \dfrac{9}{27}$?

A. $\dfrac{12}{27}$

B. $\dfrac{9}{27}$

C. $\dfrac{3}{27}$

D. $\dfrac{10}{36}$

The correct answer is A.

STEP 1: To find the LCD, you have to look at the factors for each denominator.

Factors are the numbers that equal a product when they are multiplied by each other.

So, the factors of 9 are:

1 × 9 = 9

3 × 3 = 9

The factors of 27 are:

1 × 27 = 27

3 × 9 = 27

STEP 2: Determine which factors are common to both denominators by comparing the lists of factors.

In this problem, the factors of 3 and 9 are common to the denominators of both fractions.

We can illustrate the common factors as shown.

We saw that the factors of 9 were:

1 × **9** = 9

3 × 3 = 9

The factors of 27 were:

1 × 27 = 27

3 × **9** = 27

So, the numbers in bold above are the common factors.

STEP 3: Multiply the common factors to get the lowest common denominator.

The numbers that are in bold above are then used to calculate the lowest common denominator.

3 × 9 = 27

So, the lowest common denominator (LCD) for each fraction above is 27.

STEP 4: Convert the denominator of each fraction to the LCD.

You convert the fraction by referring to the factors from step 3.

Multiply the numerator and the denominator by the same factor.

Our problem was $\dfrac{1}{9} + \dfrac{9}{27} = ?$

So, we convert the first fraction as follows:

$$\dfrac{1}{9} \times \dfrac{3}{3} = \dfrac{3}{27}$$

We do not need to convert the second fraction of $\dfrac{9}{27}$ because it already has the LCD.

STEP 5: When both fractions have the same denominator, you can perform the operation to solve the problem.

$$\frac{1}{9} + \frac{9}{27} =$$

$$\frac{3}{27} + \frac{9}{27} = \frac{12}{27}$$

Fractions – Simplifying

You will also need to know how to simplify fractions.

 A+ To simplify fractions, look to see what factors are common to both the numerator and denominator.

In the example problem above, our result was $\frac{12}{27}$.

Problem:

Simplify: $\frac{12}{27}$

A. $\frac{1}{3}$

B. $\frac{3}{4}$

C. $\frac{3}{9}$

D. $\frac{4}{9}$

The correct answer is D.

STEP 1: Look at the factors of the numerator and denominator.

The factors of 12 are:

1 × 12 = 12

2 × 6 = 12

3 × 4 = 12

You will remember that the factors of 27 are:

1 × 27 = 27

3 × 9 = 27

So, we can see that the numerator and denominator have the common factor of 3.

STEP 2: Simplify the fraction by dividing the numerator and denominator by the common factor.

Our fraction in this problem is $\dfrac{12}{27}$.

So, simplify the numerator: 12 ÷ 3 = 4

Then simplify the denominator: 27 ÷ 3 = 9

STEP 3: Use the results from step 2 to form the new fraction.

The numerator from step 2 is 4.

The denominator is 9.

So, the new fraction is $\dfrac{4}{9}$.

Mixed Numbers

Mixed numbers are those that contain a whole number and a fraction.

Convert the mixed numbers back to fractions first. Then find the lowest common denominator of the fractions in order to solve the problem.

Problem:

$$3\dfrac{1}{3} - 2\dfrac{1}{2} = ?$$

A. $\dfrac{1}{3}$

B. $\dfrac{9}{3}$

C. $\dfrac{5}{6}$

D. $1\dfrac{1}{2}$

The correct answer is C.

Our problem was: $3\dfrac{1}{3} - 2\dfrac{1}{2} = ?$

STEP 1: Convert the first mixed number to an integer plus a fraction.

$3\tfrac{1}{3} =$

$3 + \dfrac{1}{3}$

STEP 2: Then multiply the integer by a fraction whose numerator and denominator are the same as the denominator of the existing fraction.

$3 + \dfrac{1}{3} =$

$\left(3 \times \dfrac{3}{3}\right) + \dfrac{1}{3} =$

$\dfrac{9}{3} + \dfrac{1}{3}$

STEP 3: Add the two fractions to get your new fraction.

$\dfrac{9}{3} + \dfrac{1}{3} = \dfrac{10}{3}$

Then convert the second mixed number to a fraction, using the same steps that we have just completed for the first mixed number.

$2\tfrac{1}{2} =$

$2 + \dfrac{1}{2} =$

$$\left(2 \times \frac{2}{2}\right) + \frac{1}{2} =$$

$$\frac{4}{2} + \frac{1}{2} = \frac{5}{2}$$

Now that you have converted both mixed numbers to fractions, find the lowest common denominator and subtract to solve.

$$\frac{10}{3} - \frac{5}{2} =$$

$$\left(\frac{10}{3} \times \frac{2}{2}\right) - \left(\frac{5}{2} \times \frac{3}{3}\right) =$$

$$\frac{20}{6} - \frac{15}{6} =$$

$$\frac{5}{6}$$

PEMDAS – Order of Operations

The phrase "order of operations" means that you need to know which mathematical operation to do first when you are faced with longer problems.

Remember the acronym PEMDAS. "PEMDAS" means that you have to do the mathematical operations in this order:

First: Do operations inside **P**arentheses

Second: Do operations with **E**xponents

Third: Perform **M**ultiplication and **D**ivision (from left to right)

Last: Do **A**ddition and **S**ubtraction (from left to right)

Some students prefer to remember the order or operations by using the memorable phrase.

| Please Excuse My Dear Aunt Sally |

So, refer to the rules above and attempt the example problems that follow.

Problem 1:

$-6 \times 3 - 4 \div 2 = ?$

A. -20

B. -18

C. -2

D. 4

The correct answer is A.

There are no parentheses or exponents in this problem, so we need to direct our attention to the multiplication and division first.

Our problem was: $-6 \times 3 - 4 \div 2 = ?$

When you see a problem like this one, you need to do the multiplication and division from left to right.

This means that you take the number to the left of the multiplication or division symbol and multiply or divide that number on the left by the number on the right of the symbol.

So, in our problem we need to multiply -6 by 3 and then divide 4 by 2.

You can see the order of operations more clearly if you put in parentheses to group the numbers together.

$-6 \times 3 - 4 \div 2 =$

$(-6 \times 3) - (4 \div 2) =$

$-18 - 2 =$

-20

Now try a problem that has parenthesis, exponents, multiplication, division, addition, and subtraction.

Problem 2:

$$\frac{5 \times (7-4)^2 + 3 \times 8}{5 - 6 \div (4-1)} = ?$$

A. −23

B. 23

C. $\dfrac{23}{\frac{1}{3}}$

D. 128

The correct answer is B.

For this type of problem, do the operations inside the **parentheses** first.

$$\frac{5 \times (7-4)^2 + 3 \times 8}{5 - 6 \div (4-1)} =$$

$$\frac{5 \times (3)^2 + 3 \times 8}{5 - 6 \div 3}$$

Then do the operation on the **exponent**.

$$\frac{5 \times (3)^2 + 3 \times 8}{5 - 6 \div 3} =$$

$$\frac{5 \times (3 \times 3) + 3 \times 8}{5 - 6 \div 3}$$

$$\frac{5 \times 9 + 3 \times 8}{5 - 6 \div 3}$$

Then do the **multiplication** and **division**.

$$\frac{5 \times 9 + 3 \times 8}{5 - 6 \div 3} =$$

$$\frac{(5 \times 9) + (3 \times 8)}{5 - (6 \div 3)} =$$

$$\frac{45 + 24}{5 - 2}$$

Then do the **addition** and **subtraction**.

$$\frac{45 + 24}{5 - 2} = \frac{69}{3}$$

In this case, we can then simplify the fraction since both the numerator and denominator are divisible by 3.

$$\frac{69}{3} = 69 \div 3 = 23$$

Percentages and Decimals

You will have to calculate percentages and decimals on the exam, as well as use percentages and decimals to solve other types of math problems or to create equations.

Percentages can be expressed by using the symbol %. They can also be expressed as fractions or decimals.

In general, there are three ways to express percentages.

TYPE 1: Percentages as fractions

Percentages can always be expressed as the number over one hundred.

So 45% = $^{45}/_{100}$

TYPE 2: Percentages as simplified fractions

Percentages can also be expressed as simplified fractions.

In order to simplify the fraction, you have to find the largest number that will go into both the numerator and denominator.

In the case of 45%, the fraction is $^{45}/_{100}$, and the numerator and denominator are both divisible by 5.

To simplify the numerator: 45 ÷ 5 = 9.

To simplify the denominator: $100 \div 5 = 20$.

This results in the simplified fraction of $^9/_{20}$.

TYPE 3: Percentages as decimals

Percentages can also be expressed as decimals.

$45\% = {}^{45}/_{100} = 45 \div 100 = 0.45$

You may have to use these concepts in order to solve a practical problem, like the one that follows.

Problem:

Consider a class which has n students. In this class, $t\%$ of the students subscribe to digital TV packages.

Which of the following equations represents the number of students who do not subscribe to any digital TV package?

A. $100(n - t)$

B. $(100\% - t\%) \times n$

C. $(100\% - t\%) \div n$

D. $(1 - t)n$

The correct answer is B.

If $t\%$ subscribe to digital TV packages, then $100\% - t\%$ do not subscribe.

In other words, since a percentage is any given number out of 100%, the percentage of students who do not subscribe is represented by this equation:

$(100\% - t\%)$

This equation is then multiplied by the total number of students (n) in order to determine the number of students who do not subscribe to digital TV packages.

$(100\% - t\%) \times n$

Proportions

A proportion is an equation with a ratio on each side.

In other words, a proportion is a statement that two ratios are equal.

$^3/_4 = {}^6/_8$ is an example of a proportion.

We will look at ratios in more depth in the subsequent section.

 Proportions often involve simplifying fractions, which we have learned how to do in a previous section.

Proportions can be expressed as fractions, as in the following problem.

Problem:

Find the value of x that solves the following proportion: $^3/_6 = {}^x/_{14}$

A. 3

B. 6

C. 7

D. 9

The correct answer is C.

STEP 1: You can simplify the first fraction because both the numerator and denominator are divisible by 3.

$^3/_6 \div {}^3/_3 = {}^1/_2$

STEP 2: Then divide the denominator of the second fraction ($^x/_{14}$) by the denominator of the simplified fraction ($^1/_2$) from above.

$14 \div 2 = 7$

STEP 3: Now, multiply the number from step 2 by the numerator of the fraction we calculated in step 1 in order to get your result.

$1 \times 7 = 7$

You can check your answer as follows:

$$^3/_6 = {}^7/_{14}$$

$$^3/_6 \div {}^3/_3 = {}^1/_2$$

$$^7/_{14} \div {}^7/_7 = {}^1/_2$$

Ratios

Ratios take a group of people or things and divide them into two parts.

For example, if your teacher tells you that each day you should spend two hours studying math for every hour that you spend studying English, you get the ratio 2:1.

 Ratios can be expressed as fractions. Ratios can also be expressed by using the colon. For example, a ratio of 2 to 100 can be expressed as $^2/_{100}$ or 2:100.

The number before the colon expresses one subset of the total amount of items.

The number after the colon expresses a different subset of the total.

In other words, when the number before the colon and the number after the colon are added together, we have the total amount of items.

Problem:

In a shipment of 100 mp3 players, 1% are faulty.

What is the ratio of non-faulty mp3 players to faulty mp3 players?

A. 1:100

B. 99:100

C. 1:99

D. 99:1

The correct answer is D.

This problem is asking for the quantity of non-faulty mp3 players to the quantity of faulty mp3 players.

Therefore, you must put the quantity of non-faulty mp3 players before the colon in the ratio.

In this problem, 1% of the players are faulty.

1% × 100 = 1 faulty player in every 100 players

100 − 1 = 99 non-faulty players

As explained above, the number before the colon and the number after the colon can be added together to get the total quantity.

So, the ratio is 99:1.

Setting Up Basic Equations

You will see problems on the test that ask you to make mathematical equations from basic information.

| A+ | To set up an equation, read the problem carefully and then express the facts in terms of an algebraic equation. |

These types of questions are often practical problems that involve buying or selling merchandise.

Problem 1:

A company purchases cell phones at a cost of x and sells the cell phones at four times the cost.

Which of the following represents the profit made on each cell phone?

A. x

B. $3x$

C. $4x$

D. $3 − x$

The correct answer is B.

The sales price of each cell phone is four times the cost.

The cost is expressed as x, so the sales price is $4x$.

The difference between the sales price of each cell phone and the cost of each cell phone is the profit.

REMEMBER: Sales Price − Cost = Profit

In this problem, the sales price is $4x$ and the cost is x.

$4x - x$ = Profit

$3x$ = Profit

Problem 2:

An internet provider sells internet packages based on monthly rates. The price for the internet service depends on the speed of the internet connection.

The chart that follows indicates the prices of the various internet packages.

Price in dollars (P)	10	20	30	40
Gigabyte speed (s)	2	4	6	8

Which equation represents the prices of these internet packages?

A. $P = (s - 5) \times 5$

B. $P = (s + 5) \times 5$

C. $P = 5 \div s$

D. $P = s \times 5$

The correct answer is D.

The price of the internet connection is always 5 times the speed.

$10 = 2 \times 5$

$20 = 4 \times 5$

$30 = 6 \times 5$

$40 = 8 \times 5$

So, the price of the internet connection (represented by variable *P*) equals the speed (represented by variable *s*) times 5.

$P = s \times 5$

Working with Averages

Basic averages are calculated by taking the total of a data set for a group and then dividing this total by the number of people in the group.

For example, have a look at the following problem.

Three people are trying to lose weight. The first person has lost 7 pounds, the second person has lost 10 pounds, and the third person has lost 16 pounds. What is the average weight loss for this group?

STEP 1: Add all of the individual amounts together to get a total for the group.

7 + 10 + 16 = 33

STEP 2: Divide the total from step 1 by the number of people in the group.

33 ÷ 3 = 11

So, the average weight loss is 11 pounds.

However, problems with averages on the PERT Test will quite often be more difficult than the one provided above.

Problems that you see on the exam might involve an average that was calculated in error. Find the total of the data set by reversing the erroneous operation. Then divide the total by the correct number of items in order to find the correct average.

Other types of problems will give you averages for two distinct members of a group, like male and female students in a class, and then ask you to calculate the average for the entire group.

 For advanced problems on averages, multiply each average by the number of people in each group. Then add the totals for each group together and divide by the total number of people.

Problem:

120 students took a math test. The 60 female students in the class had an average score of 95, while the 60 male students in the class had an average of 90. What is the average test score for all 120 students in the class?

A. 75

B. 92.5

C. 93

D. 93.5

The correct answer is B.

STEP 1: You need to find the total points for all the females by multiplying their average by the number of female students. Then do the same to find the total points for all the males.

Females: 60 × 95 = 5700

Males: 60 × 90 = 5400

STEP 2: Then add these two amounts together to get the total for the group.

5700 + 5400 = 11,100

STEP 3: Then divide by the total number of students in the class to get your solution.

11,100 ÷ 120 = 92.5

So, the correct average is 92.5

Algebra concepts and formulas:

The algebra and college algebra parts of the exam cover:

- the FOIL method and other operations with polynomials
- factoring polynomial expressions
- fractions containing rational and radical expressions
- inequalities
- laws of exponents
- multiple solutions
- practical problems
- solving problems by substitution and elimination
- solving problems for an unknown variable
- square roots
- systems of equations

You may also see some coordinate geometry problems on the test.

That is because you need to use algebraic concepts to solve coordinate geometry problems.

Coordinate geometry is covered in the next section of the study guide.

The FOIL Method and Working with Polynomials

Polynomials are algebraic expressions that contain integers, variables, and variables which are raised to whole-number positive exponents.

You will certainly see problems involving polynomials on the PERT Test. Be sure that you know these concepts well.

Multiplying Polynomials Using the FOIL Method:

The use of the FOIL method is one of the most important things you will need to know in order to answer many of the algebra questions on the test.

A+

You will see many problems in this format on the test: $(x + y)(x + y)$.
Use the FOIL method to solve these problems, multiplying the terms in the parentheses in this order: First − Outside − Inside − Last

Look at the example algebra question below on the FOIL method. Note that there are several other problems covering this skill in the practice problems that follow this part of the study guide.

Problem:

$(3x - 2y)^2 = ?$

A. $9x^2 + 4y^2$

B. $9x^2 - 6xy^2 + 4y^2$

C. $9x^2 - 12xy + 4y^2$

D. $9x^2 + 12xy + 4y^2$

The correct answer is C.

When you see algebra questions like this one, use the FOIL method.

Study the solution below, which highlights the order to carry out the operations on the terms.

$(3x - 2y)^2 = (3x - 2y)(3x - 2y)$

FIRST: The first terms in each set of parentheses are $3x$ and $3x$: $(\textbf{3x} - 2y)(\textbf{3x} - 2y)$

$3x \times 3x = 9x^2$

OUTSIDE: The terms on the outside are $3x$ and $-2y$: (**3x** − 2y)(3x **− 2y**)

$3x \times -2y = -6xy$

INSIDE: The terms on the inside are $-2y$ and $3x$: (3x **− 2y**)(**3x** − 2y)

$-2y \times 3x = -6xy$

LAST: The last terms in each set are $-2y$ and $-2y$: (3x **− 2y**)(3x **− 2y**)

$-2y \times -2y = 4y^2$

All of these individual results are put together for your final answer to the question.

$9x^2 - 6xy - 6xy + 4y^2 =$

$9x^2 - 12xy + 4y^2$

Dividing Polynomials Using Long Division:

You may also need to perform long division on polynomials on the exam.

You can think of long division of the polynomial as reversing the FOIL operation. In other words, your result will generally be in one of the following formats: $(x + y)$ or $(x − y)$

Problem:

$(x^2 - x - 6) \div (x - 3) = ?$

A. 2x

B. x − 2

C. x − 2

D. x + 2

The correct answer is D.

In order to solve this type of problem, you must do long division of the polynomial.

Remember that you are subtracting the terms when you perform each part of the long division, so you need to be careful with negatives.

$$\begin{array}{r} x + 2 \\ x - 3 \overline{)x^2 - x - 6} \\ \underline{x^2 - 3x} \\ 2x - 6 \\ \underline{2x - 6} \\ 0 \end{array}$$

Substituting Values in Polynomial Expressions:

 A+

You may be asked to calculate the value of an expression by substituting its values. To solve these problems, put in the values for x and y and multiply. Then do the addition and subtraction.

Problem:

What is the value of the expression $4x^2 + 2xy - y^2$ when $x = 2$ and $y = -2$?

A. 4

B. 6

C. 8

D. 12

The correct answer is A.

$4x^2 + 2xy - y^2 =$

$(4 \times 2^2) + (2 \times 2 \times -2) - (-2^2) =$

$(4 \times 2 \times 2) + (2 \times 2 \times -2) - (-2 \times -2) =$

$(4 \times 4) + (2 \times -4) - (4) =$

$16 + (-8) - 4 =$

$16 - 12 = 4$

Operations on Polynomials Containing Three Terms:

You might also see problems on the exam in which you have to carry out operations on polynomial expressions that have more than two terms.

A+ If you see polynomial expressions that have more than two terms inside each set of parentheses, remember to use the distributive property of multiplication to solve the problem.

To solve these types of problems, you will also need to understand basic exponent laws.

We will look at exponents in more detail in the "Law of Exponents" section.

Problem:

Perform the operation: $(5ab - 6a)(3ab^3 - 4b^2 - 3a)$

A. $15a^2b^4 - 20ab^3 - 15a^2b - 18a^2b^3 - 24ab^2 - 18a^2$

B. $15a^2b^4 - 20ab^3 - 15a^2b - 18a^2b^3 + 24ab^2 + 18a^2$

C. $15a^2b^4 - 20ab^3 - 15a^2b - 18a^2b^3 - 24ab^2 + 18a^2$

D. $15ab^4 - 20ab^3 - 15a^2b - 18a^2b^3 + 24ab^2 + 18a^2$

The correct answer is B.

STEP 1: Apply the distributive property of multiplication by multiplying the first term in the first set of parentheses by all of the terms inside the second pair of parentheses.

Then multiply the second term from the first set of parentheses by all of the terms inside the second set of parentheses.

$(5ab - 6a)(3ab^3 - 4b^2 - 3a) =$

$(5ab \times 3ab^3) + (5ab \times -4b^2) + (5ab \times -3a) + (-6a \times 3ab^3) + (-6a \times -4b^2) + (-6a \times -3a)$

STEP 2: Add up the individual products in order to solve the problem.

$(5ab \times 3ab^3) + (5ab \times -4b^2) + (5ab \times -3a) + (-6a \times 3ab^3) + (-6a \times -4b^2) + (-6a \times -3a) =$

$15a^2b^4 - 20ab^3 - 15a^2b - 18a^2b^3 + 24ab^2 + 18a^2$

Factoring Polynomials

Factoring means that you have to break down a polynomial into smaller parts.

You can factor by looking for integers or variables that are common to all of the terms of the equation.

A+ | In order to factor an equation, you must figure out what variables are common to each term of the equation.

Basic Factoring:

Some problems will involve placing a term in front of a set of parentheses, as in the following example.

Problem:

Factor the following: $2xy - 6x^2y + 4x^2y^2$

A. $2xy(1 + 3x - 2xy)$

B. $2xy(1 - 3x + 2xy)$

C. $2xy(1 + 3x + 2xy)$

D. $2xy(1 - 3x - 2xy)$

The correct answer is B.

Looking at this equation, we can see that each term contains x. We can also see that each term contains y.

So, first factor out xy.

$2xy - 6x^2y + 4x^2y^2 =$

$xy(2 - 6x + 4xy)$

Then, think about integers. We can see that all of the terms inside the parentheses are divisible by 2.

Now let's factor out the 2. To do this, we divide each term inside the parentheses by 2.

$xy(2 - 6x + 4xy) =$

$2xy(1 - 3x + 2xy)$

Factoring – Advanced Problems:

You will also see problems like the one below that include more than one polynomial.

These types of problems often involve multiplying or dividing fractions that contain rational expressions.

 In order to factor problems containing more than one polynomial, you will need to find the factors of the terms inside each set of parentheses.

We will look at this concept again in the section entitled "Fractions Containing Rational Expressions."

Problem:

Factor the following. Then simplify. $\dfrac{x^2+5x+6}{x^2+6x+8} \times \dfrac{x^2+4x}{x^2+8x+15}$

A. $\dfrac{5}{x+5}$

B. $\dfrac{x}{x+5}$

C. $\dfrac{x+3}{x+4}$

D. $\dfrac{x+4}{x+3}$

The correct answer is B.

$$\dfrac{x^2+5x+6}{x^2+6x+8} \times \dfrac{x^2+4x}{x^2+8x+15} = ?$$

For this type of problem, first you need to find the factors of the numerators and denominators of each fraction.

When there are only addition signs in the rational expression, the factors will be in the following format:

$(\quad + \quad)(\quad + \quad)$

If there is a negative sign, then the factors will be in this format:

(+)(−)

You have to find the factors of the terms containing x or y variables, as well as the factors of the integers or other constants.

It is usually best to start with finding the factors of the final integer in each polynomial expression.

STEP 1: The numerator of the first fraction is $x^2 + 5x + 6$, so the final integer is 6.

The factors of 6 are:

1 × 6 = 6

2 × 3 = 6

Add these factors together to discover what integer you need to use in front of the second term of the expression.

1 + 6 = 7

2 + 3 = 5

2 and 3 satisfy both parts of the equation.

Therefore, the factors of $x^2 + 5x + 6$ are $(x + 2)(x + 3)$.

Now factor the other parts of the problem.

STEP 2: The denominator of the first fraction is $x^2 + 6x + 8$, so the final integer is 8.

The factors of 8 are:

1 × 8 = 8

2 × 4 = 8

Then add these factors together to find the integer to use in front of the second term of the expression.

1 + 8 = 9

2 + 4 = 6

Therefore, the factors of $x^2 + 6x + 8$ are $(x+2)(x+4)$.

STEP 3: The numerator of the second fraction is $x^2 + 4x$, so there is no final integer.

Because x is common to both terms of the expression, the factor will be in this format:

$x(x +)$

Therefore, in order to factor $x^2 + 4x$, we express it as $x(x+4)$.

STEP 4: The denominator of the second fraction is $x^2 + 8x + 15$, so the final integer is 15.

The factors of 15 are:

1 × 15 = 15

3 × 5 = 15

Add these factors together to find the integer to use in front of the second term of the expression.

1 + 15 = 16

3 + 5 = 8

Therefore, the factors of $x^2 + 8x + 15$ are $(x+3)(x+5)$.

A good shortcut for this type of problem is to remind yourself that it is a problem about factoring, so the factors you find in step 1 will probably be common to other parts of the expression.

In other words, we discovered in step 1 that the factors of $x^2 + 5x + 6$ are $(x+2)$ and $(x+3)$.

So, when you are factoring out the other parts of the problem, start with $(x+2)$ and $(x+3)$.

Now that we have completed all of the four steps above, we can set out our problem with the factors we discovered in each step.

We can see the factors of each fraction more clearly as follows:

$$\frac{x^2 + 5x + 16}{x^2 + 6x + 18} = \frac{(x+2)(x+3)}{(x+2)(x+4)} \qquad \frac{x^2 + 4x}{x^2 + 8x + 15} = \frac{x(x+4)}{(x+3)(x+5)}$$

The problem should be set up as follows after you have found the factors:

$$\frac{x^2+5x+6}{x^2+6x+8} \times \frac{x^2+4x}{x^2+8x+15} =$$

$$\frac{(x+2)(x+3)}{(x+2)(x+4)} \times \frac{x(x+4)}{(x+3)(x+5)}$$

Then you need to simplify by removing the common factors.

Remove $(x + 2)$ from the first fraction.

$$\frac{(x+2)(x+3)}{(x+2)(x+4)} \times \frac{x(x+4)}{(x+3)(x+5)} =$$

$$\frac{(x+3)}{(x+4)} \times \frac{x(x+4)}{(x+3)(x+5)}$$

Once you have simplified each fraction as much as possible, perform the operation indicated.

In this problem, we are multiplying. So, we can express the two factored-out fractions as one fraction and then remove the other common terms.

$$\frac{(x+3)}{(x+4)} \times \frac{x(x+4)}{(x+3)(x+5)} =$$

$$\frac{(x+3)(x+4)x}{(x+4)(x+3)(x+5)}$$

You can remove $(x + 3)$ from the above fraction since it is in both the numerator and denominator.

$$\frac{(x+3)(x+4)x}{(x+4)(x+3)(x+5)} =$$

$$\frac{(x+4)x}{(x+4)(x+5)}$$

We can further simplify by removing $(x +4)$.

$$\frac{(x+4)x}{(x+4)(x+5)} =$$

$$\frac{x}{(x+5)}$$

So, our final answer is $\frac{x}{x+5}$

Factoring to Find Possible Values of a Variable:

You may see problems on the exam that give you a polynomial expression and ask you to determine possible values for the variables in the expression.

A+   If you are asked to find values for variables such as x or y in a math problem, substitute zero for one variable. Then substitute zero for the other variable in order to solve the problem.

Problem:

What are two possible values of x for the following equation? $x^2 + 6x + 8 = 0$

A. 1 and 2

B. 2 and 4

C. 6 and 8

D. –2 and –4

The correct answer is D.

STEP 1: Factor the equation.

$x^2 + 6x + 8 = 0$

$(x + 2)(x + 4) = 0$

STEP 2: Now substitute 0 for x in the first pair of parentheses.

$(0 + 2)(x + 4) = 0$

$2(x + 4) = 0$

$2x + 8 = 0$

$2x + 8 - 8 = 0 - 8$

$2x = -8$

$2x \div 2 = -8 \div 2$

$x = -4$

STEP 3: Then substitute 0 for x in the second pair of parentheses.

$(x + 2)(x + 4) = 0$

$(x + 2)(0 + 4) = 0$

$(x + 2)4 = 0$

$4x + 8 = 0$

$4x + 8 - 8 = 0 - 8$

$4x = -8$

$4x \div 4 = -8 \div 4$

$x = -2$

Fractions Containing Fractions

On the college algebra part of the exam, you will see fractions that have fractions in their numerators or denominators.

 When you see fractions containing fractions, remember to treat the denominator as the division sign. Then invert the second fraction and multiply.

Problem:

$$\frac{x + \dfrac{1}{5}}{\dfrac{1}{x}} = ?$$

A. $x^2 + 5$

B. $\dfrac{x^3}{5}$

C. $x^2 + \dfrac{x}{5}$

D. $\dfrac{x + \dfrac{1}{5}}{x}$

The correct answer is C.

As stated above, the fraction can also be expressed as division.

$$\dfrac{x + \dfrac{1}{5}}{\dfrac{1}{x}} = \left(x + \dfrac{1}{5}\right) \div \dfrac{1}{x}$$

Then invert the second fraction and multiply the fractions as usual.

In this case $\dfrac{1}{x}$ becomes $\dfrac{x}{1}$ when inverted, which is then simplified to x.

$$\left(x + \dfrac{1}{5}\right) \div \dfrac{1}{x} =$$

$$\left(x + \dfrac{1}{5}\right) \times x =$$

$$x^2 + \dfrac{x}{5}$$

Fractions Containing Radicals

You may see fractions that contain radicals in the numerator or denominator.

If your problem has a fraction that contains a radical in its numerator or denominator, you need to eliminate the radical by multiplying both sides of the equation by the radical.

Problem:

If $\dfrac{30}{\sqrt{x^2 - 75}} = 6$, then $x = ?$

A. 100

B. 30

C. 25

D. 10

The correct answer is D.

Eliminate the radical in the denominator by multiplying both sides of the equation by the radical.

$$\frac{30}{\sqrt{x^2 - 75}} = 6$$

$$\frac{30}{\sqrt{x^2 - 75}} \times \sqrt{x^2 - 75} = 6 \times \sqrt{x^2 - 75}$$

$$30 = 6\sqrt{x^2 - 75}$$

Then eliminate the integer in front of the radical.

$$30 = 6\sqrt{x^2 - 75}$$

$$30 \div 6 = \left(6\sqrt{x^2 - 75}\right) \div 6$$

$$5 = \sqrt{x^2 - 75}$$

Then eliminate the radical by squaring both sides of the equation, and solve for x.

$$5 = \sqrt{x^2 - 75}$$

$$5^2 = \left(\sqrt{x^2 - 75}\right)^2$$

$$25 = x^2 - 75$$

$$25 + 75 = x^2 - 75 + 75$$

$$100 = x^2$$

$$x = 10$$

Fractions Containing Rational Expressions

On the algebra and college-level math parts of the exam, you may see fractions that contain rational expressions.

Rational expressions are math problems that contain algebraic terms.

Adding and Subtracting Fractions Containing Rational Expressions:

You may have to add or subtract two fractions that contain rational expressions.

 To add or subtract two fractions that contain rational expressions, you need to calculate the lowest common denominator, just like you would for any other problem with fractions.

Problem :

$$\frac{x^5}{x^2 - 6x} + \frac{5}{x} = ?$$

A. $\dfrac{4 + x^6}{x^2 - 3x}$

B. $\dfrac{4x^2 - 16x}{x^7}$

C. $\dfrac{x^5 + 5x + 30}{x^2 - 6x}$

D. $\dfrac{x^5 + 5x - 30}{x^2 - 6x}$

The correct answer is D.

Find the lowest common denominator. Since x is common to both denominators, we can convert the denominator of the second fraction to the LCD by multiplying by $(x - 6)$.

$$\frac{x^5}{x^2 - 6x} + \frac{5}{x} =$$

$$\frac{x^5}{x^2 - 6x} + \left(\frac{5}{x} \times \frac{x - 6}{x - 6} \right) =$$

$$\frac{x^5}{x^2 - 6x} + \frac{5x - 30}{x^2 - 6x} =$$

$$\frac{x^5 + 5x - 30}{x^2 - 6x}$$

Multiplying Fractions Containing Rational Expressions:

The following problem asks you to multiply two fractions, both of which contain rational expressions.

To multiply fractions containing rational expressions, multiply the numerator of the first fraction by the numerator of the second fraction to get the new numerator. Then multiply the denominators.

Problem:

$$\frac{2x^3}{5} \times \frac{4}{x^2} = ?$$

A. $\dfrac{8x}{5}$

B. $\dfrac{5}{8x}$

C. $\dfrac{8}{5}$

D. $8x$

The correct answer is A.

Multiply the numerator of the first fraction by the numerator of the second fraction. Then multiply the denominators.

$$\frac{2x^3}{5} \times \frac{4}{x^2} = \frac{8x^3}{5x^2}$$

Then factor the numerator and denominator.

As stated previously, we will discuss operations on exponents in more depth in the "Laws of Exponents" section of the study guide.

$$\frac{8x^3}{5x^2} = \frac{8x(x^2)}{5(x^2)}$$

Then we can cancel out x^2 to solve the problem.

$$\frac{8x(x^2)}{5(x^2)} = \frac{8x}{5}$$

Dividing Fractions Containing Rational Expressions:

You may also be asked to divide two fractions, both of which contain rational expressions.

 In order to divide fractions that contain rational expressions, invert the second fraction and multiply. Then cancel out any common factors. Be sure to cancel out completely.

Problem:

$$\frac{6x+6}{x^2} \div \frac{3x+3}{x^3} = ?$$

A. $2x$

B. $6x$

C. $18x^3$

D. $\dfrac{3x+3}{x}$

The correct answer is A.

The first step in solving the problem is to invert and multiply by the second fraction.

$$\frac{6x+6}{x^2} \div \frac{3x+3}{x^3} =$$

$$\frac{6x+6}{x^2} \times \frac{x^3}{3x+3} =$$

$$\frac{x^3(6x+6)}{x^2(3x+3)}$$

Then factor the numerator and denominator. $(x + 1)$ is common to both the numerator and the denominator, so we can factor that out.

$$\frac{x^3(6x+6)}{x^2(3x+3)} =$$

$$\frac{x^3 6(x+1)}{x^2 3(x+1)}$$

Now cancel out the $(x + 1)$.

$$\frac{x^3 6(x+1)}{x^2 3(x+1)} =$$

$$\frac{x^3 6}{x^2 3} =$$

$$\frac{6x^3}{3x^2}$$

Now factor out x^2 and cancel it out.

$$\frac{6x^3}{3x^2} =$$

$$\frac{6x \times x^2}{3x^2} =$$

$$\frac{6x}{3}$$

The numerator and denominator share the factor of 3, so cancel out further in order to get your final result.

$$\frac{6x}{3} =$$

$$\frac{3 \times 2 \times x}{3} =$$

$2x$

Inequalities

Inequality problems will have a less than or greater than sign. There may be more than one equation in a single inequality problem on the PERT exam.

When solving inequality problems, isolate integers before dealing with any fractions. Also remember that if you multiply an inequality by a negative number, you have to reverse the direction of the less than or greater than sign.

Problem 1:

$40 - \frac{3x}{5} \geq 10$, then $x \leq$?

A. 15

B. 30

C. 40

D. 50

The correct answer is D.

Deal with the whole numbers on each side of the equation first.

$$40 - \frac{3x}{5} \geq 10$$

$$(40 - 40) - \frac{3x}{5} \geq 10 - 40$$

$$-\frac{3x}{5} \geq -30$$

Then deal with the fraction.

$$-\frac{3x}{5} \geq -30$$

$$\left(5 \times -\frac{3x}{5}\right) \ge -30 \times 5$$

$$-3x \ge -30 \times 5$$

$$-3x \ge -150$$

Then deal with the remaining whole numbers.

$$-3x \ge -150$$

$$-3x \div 3 \ge -150 \div 3$$

$$-x \ge -150 \div 3$$

$$-x \ge -50$$

Then deal with the negative number.

$$-x \ge -50$$

$$-x + 50 \ge -50 + 50$$

$$-x + 50 \ge 0$$

Finally, isolate the unknown variable as a positive number.

$$-x + 50 \ge 0$$

$$-x + x + 50 \ge 0 + x$$

$$50 \ge x$$

$$x \le 50$$

Problem 2:

Inequalities may also be expressed in practical problems like the one below.

In the equations below, x represents the cost of one online game and y represents the cost of one movie ticket.

If $x - 2 > 5$ and $y = x - 2$, then the cost of 2 discounted movie tickets is greater than which one of the following?

A. $x - 2$

B. $x - 5$

C. $y + 5$

D. 10

The correct answer is D.

For problems like this, look to see if both of the equations have any variables or terms in common.

In this problem, both equations contain $x - 2$.

The cost of one movie ticket is represented by y, and y is equal to $x - 2$.

Therefore, we can substitute values from one equation to another.

$x - 2 > 5$

$y > 5$

If two tickets are being purchased, we need to solve for $2y$.

$y \times 2 > 5 \times 2$

$2y > 10$

Laws of Exponents

You will need to know exponent laws very well for the examination.

You will see questions on the exam that involve adding and subtracting exponents.

When the base numbers are the same and you need to multiply, you add the exponents. When the base numbers are the same and you need to divide, you subtract the exponents.

We can prove the above concepts as shown below.

For multiplication with a variable:

$x^4 \times x^2 = x^6$

$x^6 = x \times x \times x \times x \times x \times x$

For multiplication with an integer:

$2^3 \times 2^2 = 2^5$

$8 \times 4 = 32$

$2^5 = 2 \times 2 \times 2 \times 2 \times 2 = 32$

For division with a variable:

$y^5 \div y^3 = y^2$

$y^2 = y \times y$

For division with an integer:

$2^3 \div 2^2 = 2^1 = 2$

$8 \div 4 = 2$

Do not get confused when you are asked to add or subtract the variables or integers themselves.

Example with a variable: $x^2 + x^2 = 2x^2$

Example with integers: $2^3 + 2^2 = 8 + 4 = 12$

Now try the problems that follow.

Adding exponents:

Problem:

$11^5 \times 11^3 = ?$

A. 11^8

B. 11^{15}

C. 22^8

D. 121^8

The correct answer is A.

The base number in this example is 11.

So, we add the exponents: $5 + 3 = 8$

That is:

$11^5 \times 11^3 =$

$11^{(5 + 3)} =$

11^8

Subtracting exponents:

Problem:

$10^6 \div 10^4 = ?$

A. 10^{24}

B. 10^2

C. 20^{24}

D. 20^2

The correct answer is B.

The base number in this example is 10.

So, we subtract the exponents: $6 - 4 = 2$

$10^6 \div 10^4 =$

$10^{(6 - 4)} =$

10^2

Multiple Solutions

You will see questions on the exam that give you an equation and then ask you how many solutions there are for the equation provided.

You will need to consider both positive and negative numbers as potential solutions.

Problem 1:

How many solutions exist for the following equation?

$x^2 + 8 = 0$

A. 0

B. 1

C. 2

D. 4

The correct answer is A.

Remember that any real number squared will always equal a positive number.

Since 8 is added to the first value x^2, the result will always be 8 or greater.

In other words, since x^2 is always a positive number, the result of the equation would never be 0.

So, there are zero solutions for this equation.

Problem 2:

How many solutions exist for the following equation?

$x^2 - 9 = 0$

A. 0

B. 1

C. 2

D. 4

The correct answer is C.

Any real number squared will always equal a positive number.

Since 9 is subtracted from x^2, x^2 needs to be equal to 9.

Both 3 and −3 solve the equation. So, there are two solutions for this equation.

Practical Problems

Several questions on the PERT Test will ask you to solve practical problems.

 Practical problems may involve calculating a discount on an item in a store. Other common practical problems involve calculations with exam scores or other data for a class of students.

Now have a look at another type of practical problem, which involves knowledge of basic equations.

We will look at basic equations in more depth in the "Setting Up Basic Equations" section of this study guide.

For some basic equation problems, you will see two equations which have the same two variables, like J and T in the problem below.

Problem:

A company sells jeans and T-shirts. J represents jeans and T represents T-shirts in the equations below.

$2J + T = \$50$

$J + 2T = \$40$

Sarah buys one pair of jeans and one T-shirt. How much does she pay for her entire purchase?

A. $10

B. $20

C. $30

D. $70

The correct answer is C.

In order to solve the problem, take the second equation and isolate J on one side of the equation. By doing this, you define variable J in terms of variable T.

$J + 2T = \$40$

$J + 2T - 2T = \$40 - 2T$

$J = \$40 - 2T$

Now substitute $40 − 2T$ for variable J in the first equation to solve for variable T.

$2J + T = 50$

$2(40 − 2T) + T = 50$

$80 − 4T + T = 50$

$80 − 3T = 50$

$80 − 3T + 3T = 50 + 3T$

$80 = 50 + 3T$

$80 − 50 = 50 − 50 + 3T$

$30 = 3T$

$30 ÷ 3 = 3T ÷ 3$

$10 = T$

So, now that we know that a T-shirt costs $10, we can substitute this value in one of the equations in order to find the value for the jeans, which is variable J.

$2J + T = 50$

$2J + 10 = 50$

$2J + 10 − 10 = 50 − 10$

$2J = 40$

$2J ÷ 2 = 40 ÷ 2$

$J = 20$

Now solve for Sarah's purchase. If she purchased one pair of jeans and one T-shirt, then she paid:

$10 + $20 = $30

Solving by Elimination

When you have to solve a problem by elimination, you will see two equations as in the following question.

In order to solve by elimination, you need to subtract the second equation from the first equation.

Problem:

Solve the following by elimination.

$x + 4y = 30$

$2x + 2y = 36$

A. $x = 2$ and $y = 7$

B. $x = 4$ and $y = 14$

C. $x = 14$ and $y = 4$

D. $x = 16$ and $y = 2$

The correct answer is C.

Look at the x term of the second equation, which is $2x$.

In order to eliminate the x variable, we need to multiply the first equation by 2 and then subtract the second equation from this result.

$x + 4y = 30$

$(2 \times x) + (2 \times 4y) = (30 \times 2)$

$2x + 8y = 60$

Now subtract the two equations.

$$\begin{array}{r} 2x + 8y = 60 \\ -(2x + 2y = 36) \\ \hline 6y = 24 \end{array}$$

Then solve for y.

$6y = 24$

$6y \div 6 = 24 \div 6$

$y = 4$

Using our first equation $x + 4y = 30$, substitute the value of 4 for y to solve for x.

$x + 4y = 30$

$x + (4 \times 4) = 30$

$x + 16 = 30$

$x + 16 - 16 = 30 - 16$

$x = 14$

Solving for an Unknown Variable

You will certainly see problems involving solving equations for an unknown variable on the exam.

Perform the multiplication on the items in parentheses first. Then eliminate the integers and solve for x.

Problem:

If $3x - 2(x + 5) = -8$, then $x = $?

A. 1

B. 2

C. 3

D. 5

The correct answer is B.

To solve this type of problem, do multiplication on the items in parentheses first.

$3x - 2(x + 5) = -8$

$3x - 2x - 10 = -8$

Then deal with the integers by putting them on one side of the equation.

$3x - 2x - 10 + 10 = -8 + 10$

$3x - 2x = 2$

Then solve for *x*.

$3x - 2x = 2$

$1x = 2$

$x = 2$

Square Roots, Cube Roots, and Other Radicals

Square roots and cube roots are sometimes referred to as radicals.

You will need to know how to perform the operations of multiplication and division on square and cube roots.

You will also see problems that involve rationalizing and factoring square and cube roots.

Factoring radicals:

Factoring radicals requires the same concepts as factoring integers or polynomial expressions.

You have to find the factors of the numbers inside the square root symbols.

> In order to factor a radical, you need to find the squared factors of the number inside the radical sign. For example:
> $\sqrt{128} = \sqrt{64 \times 2} = \sqrt{8 \times 8 \times 2} = 8\sqrt{2}$

Problem 1:

Which of the answers below is equal to the following radical expression? $\sqrt{45}$

A. $1 \div 45$

B. $5\sqrt{9}$

C. $9\sqrt{5}$

D. $3\sqrt{5}$

The correct answer is D.

For square root problems like this one, you need to remember certain mathematical principles.

First, remember to factor the number inside the square root sign.

The factors of 45 are:

1 × 45 = 45

3 × 15 = 45

5 × 9 = 45

Then look to see if any of these factors have square roots that are whole numbers.

In this case, the only factor whose square root is a whole number is 9.

Now find the square root of 9.

$\sqrt{9} = 3$

Finally, you need to put this number at the front of the square root sign and put the other factor inside the square root sign in order to solve the problem.

$\sqrt{45} =$

$\sqrt{9 \times 5} =$

$\sqrt{3 \times 3 \times 5} =$

$3\sqrt{5}$

Problem 2:

You may see advanced problems on radicals involving other operations, such as addition or subtraction.

$\sqrt{32} + 2\sqrt{72} + 3\sqrt{18} = ?$

A. $2\sqrt{16} + 2\sqrt{36} + 3\sqrt{9}$

B. $5\sqrt{122}$

C. $6\sqrt{122}$

D. $25\sqrt{2}$

The correct answer is D.

First you need to find the squared factors of the amounts inside the radical signs.

In this problem, 16, 36, and 9 are squared factors of each radical because $16 = 4^2$, $36 = 6^2$, and $9 = 3^2$.

$$\sqrt{32} + 2\sqrt{72} + 3\sqrt{18} =$$

$$\sqrt{2 \times 16} + 2\sqrt{2 \times 36} + 3\sqrt{2 \times 9}$$

Then expand the amounts inside the radicals for the factors and simplify.

$$\sqrt{2 \times 16} + 2\sqrt{2 \times 36} + 3\sqrt{2 \times 9} =$$

$$\sqrt{2 \times (4 \times 4)} + 2\sqrt{2 \times (6 \times 6)} + 3\sqrt{2 \times (3 \times 3)} =$$

$$4\sqrt{2} + (2 \times 6)\sqrt{2} + (3 \times 3)\sqrt{2} =$$

$$4\sqrt{2} + 12\sqrt{2} + 9\sqrt{2} =$$

$$25\sqrt{2}$$

Multiplication of radicals:

To multiply radicals, multiply the numbers inside the square root signs. Then put this result inside a square root symbol for your answer. For example: $\sqrt{x} \times \sqrt{y} = \sqrt{xy}$

Problem:

$\sqrt{6} \times \sqrt{5} = ?$

A. $\sqrt{30}$

B. $\sqrt{11}$

C. $6\sqrt{5}$

D. $5\sqrt{6}$

The correct answer is A.

Multiply the numbers inside the square root signs first.

$6 \times 5 = 30$

Then put this result inside a square root symbol for your answer.

$\sqrt{30}$

Rationalizing radicals:

You may see problems on the exam that ask you to rationalize a number or to express a radical number as a rational number.

Perform the necessary mathematical operations in order to remove the square root symbol. This normally involves factoring in order to find square or cube roots.

Problem:

Express as a rational number: $\sqrt[3]{\dfrac{64}{125}}$

A. $\dfrac{1}{5}$

B. $\dfrac{4}{5}$

C. $\dfrac{5}{4}$

D. $\dfrac{125}{64}$

The correct answer is B.

In this problem, you have to find the cube roots of the numerator and denominator in order to eliminate the radical.

Remember that the cube root is the number which satisfies the equation when multiplied by itself two times.

$$\sqrt[3]{\frac{64}{125}} = \sqrt[3]{\frac{4\times4\times4}{5\times5\times5}} = \frac{4}{5}$$

Systems of Equations

For these problems, you will see two equations, both of which will contain *x* and *y*. In one equation, *x* and *y* will be added. In the other equation, *x* and *y* will be multiplied.

In order to solve systems of equations, look at the equation that contains multiplication first. Then find the factors of the product in the equation to solve the problem.

Problem:

What ordered pair is a solution to the following system of equations?

x + *y* = 9

xy = 20

A. (2, 7)

B. (2, 10)

C. (3, 6)

D. (4, 5)

The correct answer is D.

For questions on systems of equations like this one, you should look at the multiplication equation first.

Ask yourself, what are the factors of 20? We know that 20 is the product of the following:

1 × 20 = 20

2 × 10 = 20

$4 \times 5 = 20$

Now add each of the two factors together to solve the first equation.

$1 + 20 = 21$

$2 + 10 = 12$

$4 + 5 = 9$

(4, 5) solves both equations, so it is the correct answer.

Coordinate geometry concepts and formulas:

On the PERT Exam, you will need to know coordinate geometry for problems like:

- Calculating the slope of the line

- Determining the slope-intercept formula for given points on a graph

- Calculating the distance between two points on a graph

- Determining the midpoint between two points

- Finding x and y intercepts

Many students ask why they need to know coordinate geometry for the PERT exam, since the test is designed to cover basic mathematical and algebraic concepts.

The answer is that coordinate geometry is included on the PERT because you need to understand how to use algebraic principles in order to solve coordinate geometry problems.

So, be sure that you understand the coordinate geometry concepts in this section of the study guide before you take your exam.

Distance formula

The distance formula is used to calculate the linear distance between two points on a two-dimensional graph.

The two points are represented by the coordinates (x_1, y_1) and (x_2, y_2).

A+ | The distance formula is as follows: $d = \sqrt{(x_2 - x_1)^2 + (y_2 - y_1)^2}$

Problem:

What is the distance between (1,0) and (5,4)?

A. 4

B. 5

C. 16

D. $\sqrt{32}$

The correct answer is D.

Substitute values into the distance formula from the facts stated in the problem.

$$d = \sqrt{(x_2 - x_1)^2 + (y_2 - y_1)^2}$$

$$d = \sqrt{(5-1)^2 + (4-0)^2}$$

$$d = \sqrt{4^2 + 4^2}$$

$$d = \sqrt{16 + 16}$$

$$d = \sqrt{32}$$

Midpoints

You may be asked to calculate the midpoint of two points on a graph.

Remember that you divide the sum of the two points by 2 because the midpoint is the halfway mark between the two points on the line.

The two points are represented by the coordinates (x_1, y_1) and (x_2, y_2).

The midpoints of two points on a two-dimensional graph are calculated by using the midpoint formula: $(x_1 + x_2) \div 2 , (y_1 + y_2) \div 2$

You might see problems like the following one on the exam:

Find the coordinates (x, y) of the midpoint of the line segment on a graph that connects the points (−4, 8) and (2, −6).

However, you may also need to use the midpoint formula in practical problems, like the one that follows.

Problem:

Consider two stores in a town. The first store is a grocery store. The second is a pizza place where customers collect their pizzas after they order them online.

The grocery store is represented by the coordinates (−4, 2) and the pizza place is represented by the coordinates (2,−4).

If the grocery store and the pizza place are connected by a line segment, what is the midpoint of this line?

A. (1, 1)

B. (−1, −1)

C. (2, 2)

D. (−2, −2)

The correct answer is B.

Remember that to find midpoints, you need to use these formulas:

midpoint $x = (x_1 + x_2) \div 2$

midpoint $y = (y_1 + y_2) \div 2$

First, find the midpoint of the x coordinates for (**−4**, 2) and (**2**,−4).

midpoint $x = (x_1 + x_2) \div 2$

midpoint $x = (-4 + 2) \div 2$

midpoint $x = -2 \div 2$

midpoint $x = -1$

Then find the midpoint of the y coordinates for (−4, **2**) and (2,**−4**).

midpoint $y = (y_1 + y_2) \div 2$

midpoint $y = (2 + -4) \div 2$

midpoint $y = -2 \div 2$

midpoint $y = -1$

So, the midpoint is (−1, −1)

Slope and Slope-Intercept

Calculating slope is one of the most important skills that you will need for coordinate geometry problems on the exam.

To put it in simple language, slope is the measurement of how steep a straight line on a graph is.

Slope will be negative when the line slants upwards to the left.

On the other hand, slope will be positive when the line slants upwards to the right.

The two points are represented by the coordinates $\left(x_1, y_1\right)$ and $\left(x_2, y_2\right)$.

Slope is represented by variable m.

We can calculate slope by using the slope formula.

A+ The slope formula is as follows: $m = \dfrac{y_2 - y_1}{x_2 - x_1}$

You will sometimes be given a set of points, and then told where the line crosses the y axis.

In that case, you will also need what is known as the slope-intercept formula.

In the slope-intercept formula, m is the slope, b is the y intercept (the point at which the line crosses the y axis), and x and y are points on the graph.

A+ Here is the slope-intercept formula: $y = mx + b$

Problem:

Marta runs up and down a hill near her house. The measurements of the hill can be placed on a two-dimensional linear graph on which $x = 5$ and $y = 165$. If the line crosses the y axis at 15, what is the slope of this hill?

A. 10

B. 20

C. 30

D. 36

The correct answer is C.

Substitute the values into the formula.

$y = mx + b$

$165 = m5 + 15$

$165 - 15 = m5 + 15 - 15$

$150 = m5$

$150 \div 5 = m5 \div 5$

$30 = m$

x and y intercepts

You may also be asked to calculate x and y intercepts in plane geometry problems.

The x intercept is the point at which a line crosses the x axis of a graph.

In order for the line to cross the x axis, y must be equal to zero at that particular point of the graph.

On the other hand, the y intercept is the point at which the line crosses the y axis.

So, in order for the line to cross the y axis, x must be equal to zero at that particular point of the graph.

 For questions about x and y intercepts, substitute 0 for y in the equation provided. Then substitute 0 for x to solve the problem.

Problem:

Find the x and y intercepts of the following equation: $x^2 + 4y^2 = 64$

A. (8, 0) and (0, 4)

B. (0, 8) and (4, 0)

C. (4, 0) and (0, 8)

D. (0, 4) and (8, 0)

The correct answer is A.

Remember to substitute 0 for y in order to find the x intercept.

$x^2 + 4y^2 = 64$

$x^2 + (4 \times 0) = 64$

$x^2 + 0 = 64$

$x^2 = 64$

$x = 8$

Then substitute 0 for x in order to find the *y* intercept.

$x^2 + 4y^2 = 64$

$(0 \times 0) + 4y^2 = 64$

$0 + 4y^2 = 64$

$4y^2 \div 4 = 64 \div 4$

$y^2 = 16$

$y = 4$

So, the *y* intercept is (0, 4) and the *x* intercept is (8, 0).

PART 2 – PERT MATH PRACTICE TESTS

PERT Math Practice Test 1:

1) Two people are going to give money to a foundation for a project. Person A will provide one-half of the money. Person B will donate one-eighth of the money. What fraction represents the unfunded portion of the project?

   A) $\frac{1}{16}$

   B) $\frac{1}{8}$

   C) $\frac{1}{4}$

   D) $\frac{3}{8}$

2) A hockey team had 50 games this season and lost 20 percent of them. How many games did the team win?

   A) 8

   B) 10

   C) 20

   D) 40

3) Carmen wanted to find the average of the five tests she has taken this semester. However, she erroneously divided the total points from the five tests by 4, which gave her a result of 90. What is the correct average of her five tests?

   A) 64

   B) 72

   C) 80

   D) 90

4) Beth took a test that had 60 questions. She got 10% of her answers wrong. How many questions did she answer correctly?

   A) 6

   B) 10

   C) 50

   D) 54

5) Professor Smith uses a system of extra-credit points for his class. Extra-credit points can be offset against the points lost on an exam due to incorrect responses.

David answered 18 questions incorrectly on the exam and lost 36 points. He then earned 25 extra credit points. By how much was his exam score ultimately lowered?

A) −11

B) 11

C) 18

D) 25

6) A group of friends are trying to lose weight. Person A lost $14^3/_4$ pounds. Person B lost $20^1/_5$ pounds. Person C lost 36.35 pounds. What is the total weight loss for the group?

A) 70.475

B) 71.05

C) 71.15

D) 71.30

7) A job is shared by 4 workers, A, B, C, and D. Worker A does $^1/_6$ of the total hours. Worker B does $^1/_3$ of the total hours. Worker C does $^1/_6$ of the total hours. What fraction represents the remaining hours allocated to person D?

A) $^1/_8$

B) $^3/_8$

C) $^1/_6$

D) $^1/_3$

8) The university bookstore is having a sale. Course books can be purchased for $40 each, or 5 books can be purchased for a total of $150. How much would a student save on each book if he or she purchased 5 books?

A) 5

B) 10

C) 50

D) 90

9) One hundred students took an English test. The 55 female students in the class had an average score of 87, while the 45 male students in the class had an average of 80. What is the average test score for all 100 students in the class?

A) 82.00

B) 83.15

64

C) 83.50

D) 83.85

10) Mary needs to get $650 in donations. So far, she has obtained 80% of the money she needs. How much money does she still need?

A) $8.19

B) $13.00

C) $32.50

D) $130.00

11) The graph of $y = 8 \div (x - 4)$ is shown below.

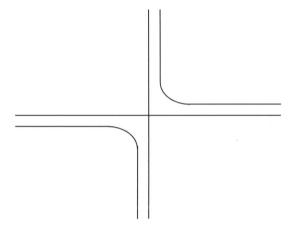

Which of the following is the best representation of $8 \div | (x - 4) |$?

A.

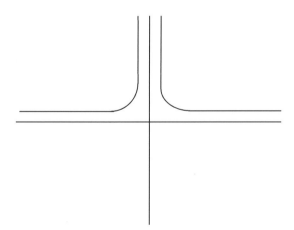

B.

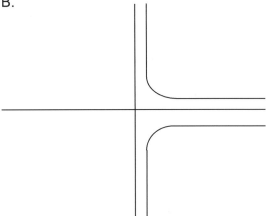

C.

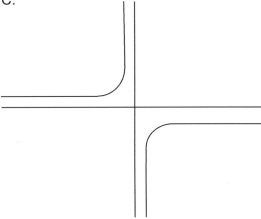

D.

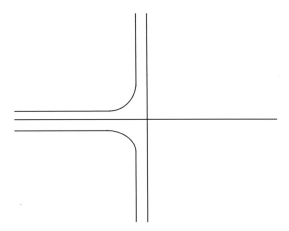

12) Which of the following is the graph of the solution set of $-3x > 6$?

A.

B.

C.

D.

13) $(x^2 - 4) \div (x + 2) = ?$

A) $x + 2$

B) $x - 2$

C) $x + 2x^2$

D) $x - x^2$

14) If $5x - 2(x + 3) = 0$, then $x = ?$

A) -2

B) -1

C) 1

D) 2

15) Simplify the following equation: $(x + 3y)^2$

A) $2(x - 3y)$

B) $2x + 6y$

C) $x^2 + 6xy - 9y^2$

D) $x^2 + 6xy + 9y^2$

16) $(x + 3y)(x - y) = ?$

A) $x^2 + 2xy - 3y^2$

B) $2x + 2xy - 2y$

C) $x^2 - 2xy + 3y^2$

D) $2x - 2xy + 2y$

17) What is the value of the expression $6x^2 - xy + y^2$ when $x = 5$ and $y = -1$?

A) 36

B) 144

C) 146

D) 156

18) Two people are going to work on a job. The first person will be paid $7.25 per hour. The second person will be paid $10.50 per hour. If A represents the number of hours the first person will work, and B represents the number of hours the second person will work, what equation represents the total cost of the wages for this job?

A) 17.75AB

B) 17.75 ÷ AB

C) AB ÷ 17.75

D) (7.25A + 10.50B)

19) $x^2 + xy - y = 41$ and $x = 5$. What is the value of y?

A) 2.6

B) 4

C) 6

D) -4

20) $20 - \dfrac{3x}{4} \geq 17$, then $x \leq ?$

A) -12

B) -4

C) –3

D) 4

21) Factor: $18x^2 - 2x$

    A) $2x(9x - 1)$

    B) $9x(2x - 1)$

    C) $2x(9x - x)$

    D) $9x(2x - x)$

22) Simplify the following: $(5x^2 + 3x - 4) - (6x^2 - 5x + 8)$

    A) $-x^2 - 2x + 4$

    B) $-x^2 - 2x - 12$

    C) $-x^2 + 8x + 4$

    D) $-x^2 + 8x - 12$

23) $(x - 4)(3x + 2) = ?$

    A) $3x^2 - 10x - 8$

    B) $3x^2 - 10x + 8$

    C) $3x^2 + 14x - 8$

    D) $3x^2 + 14x + 8$

24) Simplify: $\sqrt{7} + 2\sqrt{7}$

    A) 14

    B) $3\sqrt{7}$

    C) $2\sqrt{14}$

    D) $3\sqrt{14}$

25) Factor the following: $x^2 + x - 20$

    A) $x(x - 1) - 20$

    B) $(x - 5)(x - 4)$

    C) $(x - 5)(x + 4)$

    D) $(x + 5)(x - 4)$

26) $(x - 4y)^2 = ?$

    A) $x^2 + 16y^2$

    B) $x^2 - 8xy - 16y^2$

    C) $x^2 - 8xy + 16y^2$

    D) $x^2 + 8xy - 16y^2$

27) If $4x - 3(x + 2) = -3$, then $x = ?$

    A) 9

    B) 3

    C) 1

    D) –3

28) $(x^2 - x - 12) \div (x - 4) = ?$

    A) $(x + 3)$

    B) $(x - 3)$

    C) $(-x + 3)$

    D) $(-x - 3)$

29) Mark's final grade for a course is based on the grades from two tests, A and B. Test A counts toward 35% of his final grade. Test B counts toward 65% of his final grade. What equation is used to calculate Mark's final grade for this course?

    A) .65A + .35B

    B) .35A + .65B

    C) (.35A + .65B) ÷ 2

    D) A + B

30) What is the value of the expression $2x^2 + 3xy - y^2$ when $x = 3$ and $y = -3$?

    A) –18

    B) 0

    C) 18

    D) 36

PERT Math Practice Test 2:

1) $\sqrt{2} \times \sqrt{3} = ?$

    A) 6

    B) $\sqrt{5}$

    C) $\sqrt{6}$

    D) $\sqrt{18}$

2) Simplify: $(x - 2y)(2x - y)$

    A) $2x^2 - 3xy + 2y^2$

    B) $2x^2 + 3xy + 2y^2$

    C) $2x^2 - 5xy + 2y^2$

    D) $2x^2 - 5xy - 2y^2$

3) $20 + \dfrac{x}{4} \geq 22$, then $x \geq$?

    A) -8

    B) -2

    C) 0

    D) 8

4) State the x and y intercepts that fall on the straight line represented by the following equation:

    $y = x + 6$

    A) $(-6,0)$ and $(0,6)$

    B) $(0,6)$ and $(0,-6)$

    C) $(6,0)$ and $(0,-6)$

    D) $(0,-6)$ and $(6,0)$

5) $(5x + 7y) + (3x - 9y) = ?$

    A) $2x - 2y$

    B) $2x + 16y$

    C) $8x + 2y$

    D) $8x - 2y$

6) If $5x - 4(x + 2) = -2$, then $x = ?$

   A) 0

   B) 8

   C) 6

   D) -8

7) Simplify: $(x - y)(x + y)$

   A) x^2

   B) $x^2 - 2xy - y^2$

   C) $x^2 + 2xy - y^2$

   D) $x^2 - y^2$

8) $\sqrt{8} \times \sqrt{2} = ?$

   A) $8\sqrt{2}$

   B) $2\sqrt{8}$

   C) $\sqrt{4}$

   D) 4

9) Factor the following: $2xy - 8x^2y + 6y^2x^2$

   A) $2(xy - 4x^2y + 3x^2y^2)$

   B) $2xy(-4x + 3xy)$

   C) $2xy(1 - 4x + 3xy)$

   D) $2xy(1 + 4x - 3xy)$

10) $(x + 3) - (4 - x) = ?$

    A) -7

    B) -1

    C) $2x - 1$

    D) $2x + 1$

11) If $x - 1 > 0$ and $y = x - 1$, then $y > ?$

    A) x

    B) $x + 1$

C) $x - 1$

D) 0

12) Find the coordinates (x, y) of the midpoint of the line segment on a graph that connects the points $(-5, 3)$ and $(3, -5)$.

A) $(-1, -1)$

B) $(-1, 1)$

C) $(1, -1)$

D) $(1, 1)$

13) The price of socks is $2 per pair and the price of shoes is $25 per pair. Anna went shopping for socks and shoes, and she paid $85 in total. In this purchase, she bought 3 pairs of shoes. How many pairs of socks did she buy?

A) 2

B) 3

C) 5

D) 8

14) Consider a two-dimensional linear graph where $x = 3$ and $y = 14$. The line crosses the y axis at 5. What is the slope of this line?

A) 2.2

B) 3.0

C) 6.33

D) -2.2

15) If $5 + 5(3\sqrt{x} + 4) = 55$, then $\sqrt{x} = ?$

A) -4

B) -2

C) 2

D) 4

16) Factor the following equation: $6xy - 12x^2y - 24y^2x^2$

A) $6(xy - 2x^2y - 4x^2y^2)$

B) $xy(6 - 12x - 24xy)$

C) $6xy(-2x - 4xy)$

D) $6xy(1 - 2x - 4xy)$

17) If $x - 5 < 0$ and $y < x + 10$, then $y < ?$

A) 5

B) –5

C) 0

D) 15

18) Find the x and y intercepts of the following equation: $4x^2 + 9y^2 = 36$

A) (3,0) and (0,2)

B) (0,2) and (0,3)

C) (2,0) and (3,0)

D) (2,0) and (0,3)

19) Find the midpoint between the following coordinates: (2, 2) and (4, –6)

A) (3,4)

B) (3,–4)

C) (3,2)

D) (3,–2)

20) If $4 + 3(2\sqrt{x} - 3) = 25$, then $x = ?$

A) –5

B) –25

C) 5

D) 25

21) The Smith family is having lunch in a diner. They buy hot dogs and hamburgers to eat. The hot dogs cost $2.50 each, and the hamburgers cost $4 each. They buy 3 hamburgers. They also buy hot dogs. The total value of their purchase is $22. How many hot dogs did they buy?

A) 3

B) 4

C) 5

D) 6

22) Simplify: $(x + 5) - (x^2 - 2x)$

   A) $-x - x^2 + 5$

   B) $-x + x^2 - 5$

   C) $x - x^2 + 5$

   D) $3x - x^2 + 5$

23) $(-3x^2 + 7x + 2) - (x^2 - 5) = ?$

   A) $-2x^2 + 7x - 3$

   B) $-2x^2 + 7x + 7$

   C) $-4x^2 + 7x - 3$

   D) $-4x^2 + 7x + 7$

24) $\dfrac{x^2 + 10x + 16}{x^2 + 11x + 18} \times \dfrac{x^2 + 9x}{x^2 + 17x + 72} = ?$

   A) $\dfrac{9}{x + 9}$

   B) $\dfrac{x}{x + 9}$

   C) $\dfrac{x^2}{x^2 + 17x}$

   D) $\dfrac{x + 1}{x + 8}$

25) $\sqrt{5b - 4} = 4$ What is the value of b?

   A) 0

   B) $^5/_4$

   C) 4

   D) $^4/_5$

26) $\dfrac{5z-5}{z} \div \dfrac{6z-6}{5z^2} = ?$

A) $\dfrac{6}{25z}$

B) $\dfrac{30z^2 + 30}{5z^3}$

C) $\dfrac{6z^2 - 6z}{25z^2 - 25z}$

D) $\dfrac{25z}{6}$

27) If $c = \dfrac{a}{1-b}$, then $b = ?$

A) $\dfrac{c}{a}$

B) $\dfrac{a}{c} - 1$

C) $-\dfrac{a}{c} + 1$

D) $c - ca$

28) $\sqrt{14x^5} \times \sqrt{6x^3} = ?$

A) $\sqrt{20x^{15}}$

B) $\sqrt{84x^{15}}$

C) $2x^4\sqrt{21}$

D) $2x^8\sqrt{21}$

29) $8ab^2(3ab^4 + 2b) = ?$

A) $11a^2b^6 + 10ab^3$

B) $24a^2b^8 + 16ab^3$

C) $48ab^6 + 32ab^2$

D) $24a^2b^6 + 16ab^3$

30) Perform the operation and express as one fraction: $\dfrac{5}{12x} + \dfrac{4}{10x^2} = ?$

A) $\dfrac{9}{22x^3}$

B) $\dfrac{48x}{50x^2}$

C) $\dfrac{29}{12x}$

D) $\dfrac{25x + 24}{60x^2}$

PERT Math Practice Test 3:

1) In the standard (x, y) plane, what is the distance between $(3\sqrt{3}, -1)$ and $(6\sqrt{3}, 2)$?

    A) 6

    B) 27

    C) 36

    D) $3\sqrt{3} + 1$

2) Perform the operation: $\sqrt{5}(\sqrt{20} - \sqrt{5})$

    A) $5\sqrt{15}$

    B) $\sqrt{45}$

    C) 25

    D) 5

3) $8^7 \times 8^3 = ?$

    A) 8^4

    B) 8^{10}

    C) 8^{21}

    D) 64^{10}

4) Solve by elimination.

    $x + 5y = 24$

    $8x + 2y = 40$

    A) (4, 4)

    B) (–4, 4)

    C) (40, 4)

    D) (4, 38)

5) Perform the operation: $(4x - 3)(5x^2 + 12x + 11) = ?$

    A) $20x^3 + 33x^2 + 80x - 33$

    B) $20x^3 + 33x^2 + 80x + 33$

    C) $20x^3 + 33x^2 + 8x - 33$

    D) $20x^3 + 33x^2 - 8x - 33$

6) $\sqrt{6x^3}\sqrt{24x^5} = ?$

A) $12\sqrt{x^{15}}$

B) $\sqrt{30x^8}$

C) $12x^4$

D) $144x^4$

7) $\sqrt{18} + 3\sqrt{32} + 5\sqrt{8} = ?$

A) $17\sqrt{2}$

B) $25\sqrt{2}$

C) $8\sqrt{58}$

D) $15\sqrt{58}$

8) What equation represents the slope-intercept formula for the following data?

Through (4, 5); $m = -\dfrac{3}{5}$

A) $y = -\dfrac{3}{5}x + 5$

B) $y = -\dfrac{12}{5}x - 5$

C) $y = -\dfrac{3}{5}x - \dfrac{37}{5}$

D) $y = -\dfrac{3}{5}x + \dfrac{37}{5}$

9) For all $a \neq b$, $\dfrac{\dfrac{5a}{b}}{\dfrac{2a}{a-b}} = ?$

A) $\dfrac{10a^2}{ab - b^2}$

B) $\dfrac{a-b}{2b}$

C) $\dfrac{5a-5}{2}$

D) $\dfrac{5a-5b}{2b}$

10) Perform the operation and express as one fraction: $\dfrac{1}{a+1}+\dfrac{1}{a}$

A) $\dfrac{2}{2a+1}$

B) $\dfrac{a+1}{a}$

C) $\dfrac{a^2+a}{2a+1}$

D) $\dfrac{2a+1}{a^2+a}$

11) $\dfrac{\sqrt{48}}{3}+\dfrac{5\sqrt{5}}{6}=?$

A) $\dfrac{4\sqrt{3}+5\sqrt{5}}{6}$

B) $\dfrac{8\sqrt{3}+5\sqrt{5}}{6}$

C) $\dfrac{\sqrt{48}+5\sqrt{5}}{9}$

D) $\dfrac{6\sqrt{48}+5\sqrt{5}}{18}$

12) For all $x \neq 0$ and $y \neq 0$, $\dfrac{4x}{1/xy} = ?$

A) $\dfrac{4x}{xy}$

B) $\dfrac{xy}{4x}$

C) $\dfrac{4x}{y}$

D). $4x^2y$

13) $10a^2b^3c \div 2ab^2c^2 = ?$

A) $5c \div ab$

B) $5a \div bc$

C) $5ab \div c$

D) $5ac \div b$

14) If x and y are positive integers, the expression $\dfrac{1}{\sqrt{x} - \sqrt{y}}$ is equivalent to which of the following?

A) $\sqrt{x} - y$

B) $\sqrt{x} + y$

C) $\dfrac{\sqrt{x} - y}{1}$

D) $\dfrac{\sqrt{x} + \sqrt{y}}{x - y}$

15) $\left(2 + \sqrt{6}\right)^2 = ?$

A) 8

B) $8 + 2\sqrt{6}$

C) $8 + 4\sqrt{6}$

D) $10 + 4\sqrt{6}$

16) $\sqrt[3]{5} \times \sqrt[3]{7}$ = ?

A) $\sqrt[3]{13}$

B) $\sqrt[6]{13}$

C) $\sqrt[9]{13}$

D) $\sqrt[3]{35}$

17) What is the value of $\dfrac{x-3}{2-x}$ when $x = 1$?

A) 2

B) –2

C) $-^1/_2$

D) $-^1/_2$

18) The term PPM, pulses per minute, is used to determine how many heartbeats an individual has every 60 seconds. In order to calculate PPM, the pulse is taken for ten seconds, represented by variable P. What equation is used to calculate PPM?

A) PPM ÷ 60

B) PPM ÷ 10

C) P6

D) P10

19) Medical authorities have recommended that an individual's ideal PPM is 60. What equation is used to calculate by how much a person's PPM exceeds the ideal PPM?

A) 60 + PPM

B) 60 – PPM

C) PPM + 60

D) PPM – 60

20) A runner of a 100 mile endurance race ran at a speed of 5 miles per hour for the first 80 miles of the race and x miles per hour for the last 20 miles of the race. What equation represents the runner's average speed for the entire race?

A) $100 \div [(80 \div 5) + (20 \div x)]$

B) $100 \times [(80 \div 5) + (20 \div x)]$

C) $100 \div [(80 \times 5) + (20 \times x)]$

D) $100 \times [(80 \times 5) + (20 \times x)]$

21) $3^4 \times 3^3 = ?$

A) 9^{12}

B) 9^7

C) 6^{12}

D) 3^7

22) The number of bottles of soda that a soft drink factory can produce during D number of days using production method A is represented by the following equation:

$D^5 + 12,000$

Alternatively, the number of bottles of soda that can be produced using production method B is represented by this equation:

$D \times 10,000$

What is the largest number of bottles of soda that can be produced by the factory during a 10 day period?

A) 10,000

B) 12,000

C) 100,000

D) 112,000

23) $5^8 \div 5^2 = ?$

A) 25^6

B) 25^4

C) 5^6

D) 5^4

24) A driver travels at 60 miles per hour for two and a half hours before her car fails to start at a service station. She has to wait two hours while the car is repaired before she can continue driving. She then drives at 75 miles an hour for the remainder of her journey. She is traveling to Denver, and her journey is 240 miles in total. If she left home at 6:00 am, what time will she arrive in Denver?

A) 9:30 am

B) 11:30 am

C) 11:42 am

D) 11:50 am

25) Which one of the following is a solution to the following ordered pairs of equations?

$y = -2x - 1$

$y = x - 4$

A) (0, 1)

B) (1, -3)

C) (4, 0)

D) (1, 3)

26) At the beginning of a class, one-fourth of the students leave to attend band practice. Later, one half of the remaining students leave to go to PE. If there were 15 students remaining in the class at the end, how many students were in the class at the beginning?

A) 40

B) 45

C) 50

D) 55

27) Shania is entering a talent competition which has three events. The third event (C) counts three times as much as the second event (B), and the second event counts twice as much as the first event (A). What equation, expressed only in terms of variable A, can be used to calculate Shania's final score for the competition?

A) 2A

B) 3A

C) 6A

D) 9A

28) What ordered pair is a solution to the following system of equations?

$x + y = 11$

$xy = 24$

A) (3, 8)

B) (4, 6)

C) (2, 9)

D) (2, 12)

29) For all positive integers x and y, $x - 6 < 0$ and $y < x + 12$, then $y < ?$

A) 6

B) 12

C) 18

D) 24

30) Which of the following is the graph of the solution of $2 + y < -8$?

A.

B.

C.

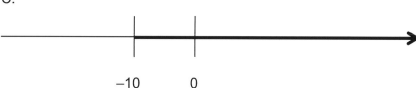

D.

ANSWERS AND SOLUTIONS TO THE PERT MATH PRACTICE TESTS

PERT Math Practice Test 1 – Answers:

1) The correct answer is D.

Two people are going to give money to a foundation for a project. Person A will provide one-half of the money. Person B will donate one-eighth of the money. What fraction represents the unfunded portion of the project?

The sum of all contributions must be equal to 100%, simplified to 1. Let's say that the variable U represents the unfunded portion of the project.

So the equation that represents this problem is $A + B + U = 1$

Substitute with the fractions that have been provided.

$$\frac{1}{2} + \frac{1}{8} + U = 1$$

For problems with fractions, you often have to find the lowest common denominator.

Finding the lowest common denominator means that you have to make all of the numbers on the bottoms of the fractions the same.

Remember that you need to find the common factors of the denominators in order to find the LCD.

We know that 2 and 4 are factors of 8.

So, the LCD for this question is 8 since the denominator of the first fraction is 2 and because 2 × 4 = 8.

So, we put the fractions into the LCD as follows:

$$\frac{1}{2} + \frac{1}{8} + U = 1$$

$$\left(\frac{1}{2} \times \frac{4}{4}\right) + \frac{1}{8} + U = 1$$

$$\frac{4}{8} + \frac{1}{8} + U = 1$$

$$\frac{5}{8} + U = 1$$

$$\frac{5}{8} - \frac{5}{8} + U = 1 - \frac{5}{8}$$

$$U = 1 - \frac{5}{8}$$

$$U = \frac{8}{8} - \frac{5}{8}$$

$$U = \frac{3}{8}$$

2) The correct answer is D.

A hockey team had 50 games this season and lost 20 percent of them. How many games did the team win?

For practical problems like this, you must first determine the percentage and formula that you need in order to solve the problem.

Then, you must do long multiplication to determine how many games the team won.

Be careful. The question tells you the percentage of games the team lost, not won.

So, first of all, we have to calculate the percentage of games won.

If the team lost 20 percent of the games, we know that the team won the remaining 80 percent.

Now do the long multiplication.

```
  50  games in total
× .80  percentage of games won (in decimal form)
 40.0  total games won
```

3) The correct answer is B.

Carmen wanted to find the average of the five tests she has taken this semester. However, she erroneously divided the total points from the five tests by 4, which gave her a result of 90. What is the correct average of her five tests?

First you need to find the total points that Carmen earned. You do this by taking Carmen's erroneous average times 4.

$4 \times 90 = 360$

Then you need to divide the total points earned by the correct number of tests in order to get the correct average.

$360 \div 5 = 72$

4) The correct answer is D.

Beth took a test that had 60 questions. She got 10% of her answers wrong. How many questions did she answer correctly?

You must first determine the percentage of questions that Beth answered correctly.

We know that she got 10% of the answers wrong, so therefore the remaining 90% were correct.

Now we multiply the total number of questions by the percentage of correct answers.

$60 \times 90\% = 54$

5) The correct answer is B.

Professor Smith uses a system of extra-credit points for his class. Extra-credit points can be offset against the points lost on an exam due to incorrect responses. David answered 18 questions incorrectly on the exam and lost 36 points. He then earned 25 extra credit points. By how much was his exam score ultimately lowered?

Take the number of questions missed and add the extra credit points.

$-36 + 25 = -11$

Since the question is asking how much the score was lowered, you need to give the amount as a positive number.

6) The correct answer is D.

A group of friends are trying to lose weight. Person A lost $14^{3}/_{4}$ pounds. Person B lost $20^{1}/_{5}$ pounds. Person C lost 36.35 pounds. What is the total weight loss for the group?

Convert the fractions in the mixed numbers to decimals.

$^{3}/_{4} = 3 \div 4 = 0.75$

$^1/_5 = 1 \div 5 = 0.20$

Then represent the mixed numbers as decimal numbers

Person 1: $14^3/_4 = 14.75$

Person 2: $20^1/_5 = 20.20$

Person 3: 36.35

Then add all three amounts together to find the total.

14.75 + 20.20 + 36.35 = 71.30

7) The correct answer is D.

A job is shared by 4 workers, A, B, C, and D. Worker A does $^1/_6$ of the total hours. Worker B does $^1/_3$ of the total hours. Worker C does $^1/_6$ of the total hours. What fraction represents the remaining hours allocated to person D?

The sum of the work from all four people must be equal to 100%, simplified to 1. In other words, they make up the total hours by working together.

A + B + C + D = 1

$^1/_6 + ^1/_3 + ^1/_6 + D = 1$

Now find the lowest common denominator of the fractions.

3 × 2 = 6, so the lowest common denominator is 6.

The fractions for Person A and Person C already have 6 in their denominators, so we only have to convert the fraction for Person B.

Convert the fraction as required.

$^1/_3 \times ^2/_2 = ^2/_6$

Now add the fractions together.

$^1/_6 + ^2/_6 + ^1/_6 + D = 1$

$^4/_6 + D = 1$

$^4/_6 - ^4/_6 + D = 1 - ^4/_6$

$D = 1 - \frac{4}{6}$

$D = \frac{2}{6}$

$D = \frac{1}{3}$

8) The correct answer is B.

The university bookstore is having a sale. Course books can be purchased for $40 each, or 5 books can be purchased for a total of $150. How much would a student save on each book if he or she purchased 5 books?

First divide the total price for the multi-purchase by the number of items.

In this case, $150 ÷ 5 = $30 for each of the five books.

Then, subtract this amount from the original price to get your answer.

$40 − $30 = $10

Alternatively, you can use the method explained below.

Calculate the total price for the five books without the discount.

5 × $40 = $200

Then subtract the discounted price of $150 from the total.

$200 - $150 = $50

Then divide the total savings by the number of books to determine the savings on each book.

$50 total savings ÷ 5 books = $10 savings per book

9) The correct answer is D.

One hundred students took an English test. The 55 female students in the class had an average score of 87, while the 45 male students in the class had an average of 80. What is the average test score for all 100 students in the class?

First of all, you have to calculate the total amount of points earned by the entire class.

Multiply the female average by the amount of female students.

Total points for female students: 87 × 55 = 4785

Then multiply the male average by the amount of male students.

Total points for male students: 80 × 45 = 3600

Then add these two amounts together to find out the total points scored by the entire class.

Total points for entire class: 4785 + 3600 = 8385

When you have calculated the total amount of points for the entire class, you divide this by the total number of students in the class to get the class average.

8385 ÷ 100 = 83.85

10) The correct answer is D.

Mary needs to get $650 in donations. So far, she has obtained 80% of the money she needs. How much money does she still need?

We know that Mary has already gotten 80% of the money.

However, the question is asking how much money she still needs.

So, 100% − 80% = 20% and 20% = .20

Now do the multiplication.

650 ×.20 = 130

11) The correct answer is A.

We know from the original graph in the question that when x is a positive number, then y will also be positive. This is represented by the curve in the upper right-hand quadrant of the graph.

We also know from the original graph in the question that when x is negative, y will also be negative. This is represented by the curve in the lower left-hand quadrant of the graph.

If we add the absolute value symbols to the problem, then $| (x - 4) |$ will always result in a positive value for y.

Therefore, even when x is negative, y will be positive.

So, the curve originally represented in the lower left-hand quadrant of the graph must be shift into the upper left-hand quadrant.

12) The correct answer is B.

Isolate the unknown variable in order to solve the problem.

$-3x > 6$

$-3x \div 3 > 6 \div 3$

$-x > 2$

In order to solve the problem, we have to multiply each side of the equation by -1.

When we multiply both sides of an inequality by a negative number, we have to reverse the greater than symbol to a less than symbol (or if there is a less than symbol, we reverse it to a greater than symbol).

$-x \times -1 < 2 \times -1$

$x < -2$

In other words, if the isolated variable is negative as in this problem, you need to reverse the greater than symbol in order to make it the less than symbol.

$-x > 2$

$x < -2$

This is represented by line B.

13) The correct answer is B.

$(x^2 - 4) \div (x + 2) = ?$

First, look at the integers in the equation. In this problem the integers are -4 and 2.

We know that we have to divide -4 by 2 because the dividend is $(x + 2)$.

$-4 \div 2 = -2$

We also know that we have to divide x^2 by x, because these are the first terms in each set of parentheses.

$x^2 \div x = x$

Now combine the two parts.

$-2 + x = x - 2$

Check your result by doing long division of the polynomial.

$$
\begin{array}{r}
x - 2 \\
x + 2 \overline{)x^2 \quad\;\; - 4} \\
\underline{x^2 + 2x} \\
-2x - 4 \\
\underline{-2x - 4} \\
0
\end{array}
$$

14) The correct answer is D.

If $5x - 2(x + 3) = 0$, then $x = $?

To solve this type of problem, do the multiplication on the items in parentheses first.

$5x - 2(x + 3) = 0$

$5x - 2x - 6 = 0$

Then deal with the integers by putting them on one side of the equation as follows:

$5x - 2x - 6 + 6 = 0 + 6$

$3x = 6$

Then solve for x.

$3x = 6$

$x = 6 \div 3$

$x = 2$

15) The correct answer is D.

Simplify the following equation: $(x + 3y)^2$

This type of algebraic expression is known as a polynomial.

When multiplying polynomials, you should use the FOIL method.

This means that you multiply the terms two at a time from each of the two parts of the equation in this order:

First – Outside – Inside – Last

$(x + 3y)^2 = (x + 3y)(x + 3y)$

FIRST – Multiply the first term from the first set of parentheses with the first term from the second set of parentheses.

$(\boldsymbol{x} + 3y)(\boldsymbol{x} + 3y)$

$x \times x = x^2$

OUTSIDE – Multiply the first term from the first set of parentheses with the second term from the second set of parentheses.

$(\boldsymbol{x} + 3y)(x + \boldsymbol{3y})$

$x \times 3y = 3xy$

INSIDE – Multiply the second term from the first set of parentheses with the first term from the second set of parentheses.

$(x + \boldsymbol{3y})(\boldsymbol{x} + 3y)$

$3y \times x = 3xy$

LAST– Multiply the second term from the first set of parentheses with the second term from the second set of parentheses.

$(x + \boldsymbol{3y})(x + \boldsymbol{3y})$

$3y \times 3y = 9y^2$

Then we add all of the above products together to get the answer.

$x^2 + 3xy + 3xy + 9y^2 =$

$x^2 + 6xy + 9y^2$

16) The correct answer is A.

$(x + 3y)(x - y) = ?$

Remember to use the FOIL method when you multiply.

As you will see below, if a term or variable is subtracted within the parentheses, you have to keep the negative sign with it when you multiply.

FIRST: $(\boldsymbol{x} + 3y)(\boldsymbol{x} - y)$

$x \times x = x^2$

OUTSIDE: $(\boldsymbol{x} + 3y)(x - \boldsymbol{y})$

$x \times -y = -xy$

INSIDE: $(x + \boldsymbol{3y})(\boldsymbol{x} - y)$

$3y \times x = 3xy$

LAST: $(x + \boldsymbol{3y})(x - \boldsymbol{y})$

$3y \times -y = -3y^2$

Then add all of the above once you have completed FOIL.

$x^2 - xy + 3xy - 3y^2 =$

$x^2 + 2xy - 3y^2$

17) The correct answer is D.

What is the value of the expression $6x^2 - xy + y^2$ when $x = 5$ and $y = -1$?

To solve this problem, put in the values for x and y and multiply. Remember that two negatives together make a positive.

For example, $-(-5) = 5$

So, be careful when multiplying negative numbers.

$6x^2 - xy + y^2 =$

$(6 \times 5^2) - (5 \times -1) + (-1^2) =$

$(6 \times 5 \times 5) - (-5) + 1 =$

$(6 \times 25) + 5 + 1 =$

$150 + 5 + 1 = 156$

18) The correct answer is D.

Two people are going to work on a job. The first person will be paid $7.25 per hour. The second person will be paid $10.50 per hour. If A represents the number of hours the first person will work, and B represents the number of hours the second person will work, what equation represents the total cost of the wages for this job?

The two people are working at different costs per hour, so each person needs to be assigned a variable.

A is for the number of hours for the first person, and B is for the number of hours for the second person.

The cost for each person is calculated by taking the number of hours that the person works by the hourly wage for that person.

So, the equation for wages for the first person is (7.25 × A)

The equation for the wages for the second person is (10.50 × B)

The total cost of the wages for this job is the sum of the wages of these two people.

(7.25 × A) + (10.50 × B) =

(7.25A + 10.50B)

19) The correct answer is B.

$x^2 + xy - y = 41$ and $x = 5$. What is the value of y?

Questions like this are just a different type of "solving by elimination" question.

Substitute 5 for the value of x to solve.

$x^2 + xy - y = 41$

$5^2 + 5y - y = 41$

$25 + 5y - y = 41$

$25 - 25 + 5y - y = 41 - 25$

$5y - y = 16$

$4y = 16$

$4y \div 4 = 16 \div 4$

$y = 4$

20) The correct answer is D.

$$20 - \frac{3x}{4} \geq 17, \text{ then } x \leq ?$$

In order to solve inequalities, deal with the whole numbers on each side of the equation first.

$$20 - \frac{3x}{4} \geq 17$$

$$(20 - 20) - \frac{3x}{4} \geq 17 - 20$$

$$-\frac{3x}{4} \geq -3$$

Then deal with the fraction.

$$-\frac{3x}{4} \geq -3$$

$$\left(4 \times -\frac{3x}{4}\right) \geq -3 \times 4$$

$$-3x \geq -12$$

Then deal with the remaining whole numbers.

$$-3x \geq -12$$

$$-3x \div 3 \geq -12 \div 3$$

$$-x \geq -4$$

Then deal with the negative number.

$$-x \geq -4$$

$$-x + 4 \geq -4 + 4$$

$$-x + 4 \geq 0$$

Finally, isolate the unknown variable as a positive number.

$-x + 4 \geq 0$

$-x + x + 4 \geq 0 + x$

$4 \geq x$

$x \leq 4$

21) The correct answer is A.

Factor: $18x^2 - 2x$

Remember that you see several factoring problems on the test.

You have to find the greatest common factor.

The factors of 18 are:

1 × 18 = 18

2 × 9 = 18

3 × 6 = 18

The factors of 2 are:

1 × **2** = 2

So, put the integer for the common factor on the outside of the parentheses.

$18x^2 - 2x = 2(\quad)$

Then put the correct values into the parentheses.

$18x^2 - 2x = 2(9x^2 - x)$

Now determine whether there are any common variables for the terms that remain in the parentheses.

So, for $(9x^2 - x)$ we can see that $9x^2$ and x have the variable x in common.

Now factor out x to solve.

$2(9x^2 - x) =$

$2x(9x - 1)$

22) The correct answer is D.

Simplify the following: $(5x^2 + 3x - 4) - (6x^2 - 5x + 8)$

Remember to perform the operations on the parentheses first and to be careful with negatives.

$(5x^2 + 3x - 4) - (6x^2 - 5x + 8) =$

$5x^2 + 3x - 4 - 6x^2 + 5x - 8$

Then place the terms containing x and y together.

$5x^2 - 6x^2 + 3x + 5x - 4 - 8$

Finally add or subtract the terms.

$5x^2 - 6x^2 + 3x + 5x - 4 - 8 =$

$-x^2 + 8x - 12$

23) The correct answer is A.

$(x - 4)(3x + 2) = ?$

This is another application of the FOIL method.

FIRST: $(\mathbf{x} - 4)(\mathbf{3x} + 2)$

$x \times 3x = 3x^2$

OUTSIDE: $(\mathbf{x} - 4)(3x + \mathbf{2})$

$x \times 2 = 2x$

INSIDE: $(x - \mathbf{4})(\mathbf{3x} + 2)$

$-4 \times 3x = -12x$

LAST: $(x - \mathbf{4})(3x + \mathbf{2})$

$-4 \times 2 = -8$

Then add all of the above once you have completed FOIL.

$3x^2 + 2x + - 12x + -8 =$

$3x^2 + 2x - 12x - 8 =$

$3x^2 - 10x - 8$

24) The correct answer is B.

Simplify: $\sqrt{7} + 2\sqrt{7}$

In order to add square roots like this, you need to add the numbers in front of the square root sign.

If there is no number before the radical, then put in the number 1 because the radical will count only 1 time in that case.

$\sqrt{7} + 2\sqrt{7} =$

$1\sqrt{7} + 2\sqrt{7} =$

$3\sqrt{7}$

25) The correct answer is D.

Factor the following: $x^2 + x - 20$

This is a reverse FOIL type of problem.

For any problem like this, the answer will be in the following format: $(x + ?)(x - ?)$

We know that the terms in the parentheses have to be in that format because we can get a negative number, like −20 above, only if we multiply a negative number and a positive number.

Next, we will look at the factors of 20:

$1 \times 20 = 20$

$2 \times 10 = 20$

$4 \times 5 = 20$

So, we know that we need to have a plus sign in one set of parentheses and a minus sign in the other set of parentheses because 20 is negative.

We also know that the factors of 20 need to be one number different than each other because the middle term is x, in other words $1x$.

The only factors of twenty that meet this criterion are 4 and 5.

Therefore the answer is $(x + 5)(x - 4)$.

26) The correct answer is C.

$(x - 4y)^2 = ?$

Here is another opportunity to practice the FOIL method.

$(x - 4y)^2 = (x - 4y)(x - 4y)$

FIRST: $(\boldsymbol{x} - 4y)(\boldsymbol{x} - 4y)$

$x \times x = x^2$

OUTSIDE: $(\boldsymbol{x} - 4y)(x - \boldsymbol{4y})$

$x \times -4y = -4xy$

INSIDE: $(x - \boldsymbol{4y})(\boldsymbol{x} - 4y)$

$-4y \times x = -4xy$

LAST: $(x - \boldsymbol{4y})(x - \boldsymbol{4y})$

$-4y \times -4y = 16y^2$

SOLUTION:

$x^2 - 8xy + 16y^2$

27) The correct answer is B.

If $4x - 3(x + 2) = -3$, then $x = ?$

Remember to do multiplication on the items in parentheses first.

$4x - 3(x + 2) = -3$

$4x - 3x - 6 = -3$

Then deal with the integers.

$4x - 3x - 6 + 6 = -3 + 6$

$4x - 3x = 3$

Then solve for x.

$4x - 3x = 3$

$x = 3$

28) The correct answer is A.

$(x^2 - x - 12) \div (x - 4) = ?$

In order to solve the problem, you have to do long division of the polynomial.

$$
\begin{array}{r}
x + 3 \\
x - 4{\overline{\smash{\big)}\,x^2 - x - 12}} \\
\underline{x^2 - 4x} \\
3x - 12 \\
\underline{3x - 12} \\
0
\end{array}
$$

29) The correct answer is B.

Mark's final grade for a course is based on the grades from two tests, A and B. Test A counts toward 35% of his final grade. Test B counts toward 65% of his final grade. What equation is used to calculate Mark's final grade for this course?

The two tests are being given different percentages, so each test needs to have its own variable.

A for test A and B for test B.

Since A counts for 35% of the final grade, we set 35% to a decimal and put the decimal in front of the variable so that the variable will have the correct weight.

So, the value of test A is .35A

Test B counts for 65%, so the value of test B is .65B

The final grade is the sum of the values for the two tests.

So, we add the above products together to get our equation.

.35A + .65B

30) The correct answer is A.

What is the value of the expression $2x^2 + 3xy - y^2$ when $x = 3$ and $y = -3$?

Put in the values for x and y and multiply.

$2x^2 + 3xy - y^2 =$

$(2 \times 3^2) + (3 \times 3 \times -3) - (-3^2) =$

$(2 \times 3 \times 3) + (3 \times 3 \times -3) - (-3 \times -3) =$

$(2 \times 9) + (3 \times -9) - (9) =$

$18 + (-27) - 9 =$

$18 - 27 - 9 =$

$18 - 36 =$

-18

PERT Math Practice Test 2 – Answers:

1) The correct answer is C.

$$\sqrt{2} \times \sqrt{3} = ?$$

In order to multiply two square roots, multiply the numbers inside the square roots.

$2 \times 3 = 6$

Then put this result inside a square root symbol for your answer.

$$\sqrt{6}$$

2) The correct answer is C.

Simplify: $(x - 2y)(2x - y)$

Do not the word "simplify" confuse you. Just apply the FOIL method again.

FIRST: $(\boldsymbol{x} - 2y)(\boldsymbol{2x} - y)$

$x \times 2x = 2x^2$

OUTSIDE: $(\boldsymbol{x} - 2y)(2x - \boldsymbol{y})$

$x \times -y = -xy$

INSIDE: $(x - \boldsymbol{2y})(\boldsymbol{2x} - y)$

$-2y \times 2x = -4xy$

LAST: $(x - \boldsymbol{2y})(2x - \boldsymbol{y})$

$-2y \times -y = 2y^2$

SOLUTION:

$2x^2 + - xy + - 4xy + 2y^2 =$

$2x^2 - xy - 4xy + 2y^2 =$

$2x^2 - 5xy + 2y^2$

3) The correct answer is D.

$20 + \dfrac{x}{4} \geq 22$, then $x \geq$?

Deal with the whole numbers first.

$$20 + \frac{x}{4} \geq 22$$

$$20 - 20 + \frac{x}{4} \geq 22 - 20$$

$$\frac{x}{4} \geq 2$$

Then eliminate the fraction.

$$\frac{x}{4} \geq 2$$

$$4 \times \frac{x}{4} \geq 2 \times 4$$

$$x \geq 8$$

4) The correct answer is A.

State the x and y intercepts that fall on the straight line represented by the following equation:

$y = x + 6$

Remember that the y intercept exists where the line crosses the y axis, so $x = 0$ for the y intercept.

Begin by substituting 0 for x.

$y = x + 6$

$y = 0 + 6$

$y = 6$

Therefore, the coordinates (0, 6) represent the y intercept.

On the other hand, the x intercept exists where the line crosses the x axis, so $y = 0$ for the x intercept.

Now substitute 0 for y.

$y = x + 6$

$0 = x + 6$

$0 - 6 = x + 6 - 6$

$-6 = x$

So, the coordinates $(-6, 0)$ represent the x intercept.

5) The correct answer is D.

$(5x + 7y) + (3x - 9y) = ?$

First perform the operations on the parentheses.

$(5x + 7y) + (3x - 9y) =$

$5x + 7y + 3x - 9y$

Then place the x and y terms together.

$5x + 7y + 3x - 9y =$

$5x + 3x + 7y - 9y$

Finally add and subtract to simplify.

$5x + 3x + 7y - 9y =$

$8x - 2y$

6) The correct answer is C.

If $5x - 4(x + 2) = -2$, then $x = ?$

Isolate the x variable in order to solve the problem.

$5x - 4(x + 2) = -2$

$5x - 4x - 8 = -2$

$x - 8 = -2$

$x - 8 + 8 = -2 + 8$

$x = 6$

7) The correct answer is D.

Simplify: $(x - y)(x + y)$

Remember to use FOIL when the instructions tell you to simplify.

FIRST: $(\boldsymbol{x} - y)(\boldsymbol{x} + y)$

$x \times x = x^2$

OUTSIDE: $(\boldsymbol{x} - y)(x + \boldsymbol{y})$

$x \times y = xy$

INSIDE: $(x - \boldsymbol{y})(\boldsymbol{x} + y)$

$-y \times x = -xy$

LAST: $(x - \boldsymbol{y})(x + \boldsymbol{y})$

$-y \times y = -y^2$

SOLUTION:

$x^2 + xy + - xy - y^2 =$

$x^2 - y^2$

8) The correct answer is D.

$\sqrt{8} \times \sqrt{2} = ?$

For radical problems like this one, remember that you have to multiply the numbers inside the square roots.

$8 \times 2 = 16$

Put this result inside a square root symbol, and then simplify, if possible.

$\sqrt{16} = 4$

9) The correct answer is C.

Factor the following: $2xy - 8x^2y + 6y^2x^2$

First, figure out what variables are common to each term of the equation.

Let's look at the equation again.

$2xy - 8x^2y + 6y^2x^2$

We can see that each term contains x. We can also see that each term contains y.

So, now let's factor out xy.

$2xy - 8x^2y + 6y^2x^2 =$

$xy(2 - 8x + 6xy)$

Then, think about integers. We can see that all of the terms inside the parentheses are divisible by 2.

Now let's factor out the 2. In order to do this, we divide each term inside the parentheses by 2.

$xy(2 - 8x + 6xy) =$

$2xy(1 - 4x + 3xy)$

10) The correct answer is C.

$(x + 3) - (4 - x) = ?$

This question is asking you to simplify the variables in the parentheses.

Do the operation on the second set of parentheses first.

$(x + 3) - (4 - x) =$

$x + 3 - 4 + x$

Now simplify for the common terms.

$x + 3 - 4 + x =$

$x + x + 3 - 4 =$

$2x - 1$

11) The correct answer is D.

If $x - 1 > 0$ and $y = x - 1$, then $y > ?$

Notice that both equations contain $x - 1$. Since the second equation has the equal sign, we can substitute y for $x - 1$ in the first equation.

$x - 1 > 0$

$x - 1 = y$

$y > 0$

12) The correct answer is A.

Find the coordinates (x, y) of the midpoint of the line segment on a graph that connects the points $(-5, 3)$ and $(3, -5)$.

Remember that in order to find midpoints on a line, you need to use the midpoint formula.

For two points on a graph (x_1, y_1) and (x_2, y_2), the midpoint is:

$(x_1 + x_2) \div 2$, $(y_1 + y_2) \div 2$

$(-5 + 3) \div 2 = $ midpoint x, $(3 + -5) \div 2 = $ midpoint y

$-2 \div 2 = $ midpoint x, $-2 \div 2 = $ midpoint y

$-1 = $ midpoint x, $-1 = $ midpoint y

13) The correct answer is C.

The price of socks is $2 per pair and the price of shoes is $25 per pair. Anna went shopping for socks and shoes, and she paid $85 in total. In this purchase, she bought 3 pairs of shoes. How many pairs of socks did she buy?

Remember to assign a different variable to each item.

Then make your equation by multiplying each variable by its price.

So, let's say that the number of pairs of socks is S and the number of pairs of shoes is H.

Your equation is:

$(S \times \$2) + (H \times \$25) = \$85$

We know that the number of pairs of shoes is 3, so put that in the equation and solve it.

$(S \times \$2) + (H \times \$25) = \$85$

$(S \times \$2) + (3 \times \$25) = \$85$

$(S \times \$2) + \$75 = \$85$

$(S \times \$2) + 75 - 75 = \$85 - \$75$

$(S \times \$2) = \$10$

$\$2S = \$10$

$\$2S \div 2 = \$10 \div 2$

$S = 5$

So, she bought 5 pairs of socks.

14) The correct answer is B.

Consider a two-dimensional linear graph where $x = 3$ and $y = 14$. The line crosses the y axis at 5. What is the slope of this line?

When you are provided with a set of coordinates and the y intercept, you need the slope-intercept formula in order to calculate the slope of a line.

$y = mx + b$

In the slope-intercept formula, m is the slope and b is the y intercept, which is the point where the line crosses the y axis.

Now solve for the numbers given in the problem.

$y = mx + b$

$14 = m3 + 5$

$14 - 5 = m3 + 5 - 5$

$9 = m3$

$9 \div 3 = m$

$3 = m$

15) The correct answer is C.

If $5 + 5(3\sqrt{x} + 4) = 55$, then $\sqrt{x} = ?$

First, deal with the integers that are outside the parentheses.

$5 + 5(3\sqrt{x} + 4) = 55$

$5 + 15\sqrt{x} + 20 = 55$

$25 + 15\sqrt{x} = 55$

$25 - 25 + 15\sqrt{x} = 55 - 25$

$15\sqrt{x} = 30$

Then divide in order to isolate $\sqrt{x}$.

$15\sqrt{x} = 30$

$(15\sqrt{x}) \div 15 = 30 \div 15$

$\sqrt{x} = 2$

16) The correct answer is D.

Factor the following equation: $6xy - 12x^2y - 24y^2x^2$

Remember to ask yourself: What variables are common to each term of the equation?

We can see that each term contains x. We can also see that each term contains y.

So, now let's factor out xy.

$6xy - 12x^2y - 24y^2x^2 =$

$xy(6 - 12x - 24xy)$

Then, think about integers. We can see that all of the terms inside the parentheses are divisible by 6.

So, factor out the 6 by dividing each term inside the parentheses by 6.

$xy(6 - 12x - 24xy) =$

$6xy(1 - 2x - 4xy)$

17) The correct answer is D.

If $x - 5 < 0$ and $y < x + 10$, then $y < ?$

First solve the equation for x.

$x - 5 < 0$

$x - 5 + 5 < 0 + 5$

$x < 5$

Then solve for y by replacing x with its value.

$y < x + 10$

$y < 5 + 10$

$y < 15$

18) The correct answer is A.

Find the x and y intercepts of the following equation: $4x^2 + 9y^2 = 36$

Remember that for questions about x and y intercepts, you need to substitute 0 for x and then substitute 0 for y in order to solve the problem.

Here is the solution for y intercept:

$4x^2 + 9y^2 = 36$

$4(0x^2) + 9y^2 = 36$

$0 + 9y^2 = 36$

$9y^2 \div 9 = 36 \div 9$

$y^2 = 4$

$y = 2$

So, the y intercept is $(0, 2)$

Here is the solution for x intercept:

$4x^2 + 9y^2 = 36$

$4x^2 + 9(0y^2) = 36$

$4x^2 + 0 = 36$

$4x^2 \div 4 = 36 \div 4$

$x^2 = 9$

$x = 3$

So the x intercept is (3, 0)

19) The correct answer is D.

Find the midpoint between the following coordinates: (2, 2) and (4, –6)

Use the midpoint formula.

For two points on a graph (x_1, y_1) and (x_2, y_2), the midpoint is:

$(x_1 + x_2) \div 2$, $(y_1 + y_2) \div 2$

$(2 + 4) \div 2$ = midpoint x, $(2 - 6) \div 2$ = midpoint y

$6 \div 2$ = midpoint x, $-4 \div 2$ = midpoint y

3 = midpoint x, –2 = midpoint y

20) The correct answer is D.

If $4 + 3(2\sqrt{x} - 3) = 25$, then x = ?

Deal with the integers that are outside the parentheses first.

$4 + 3(2\sqrt{x} - 3) = 25$

$4 - 4 + 3(2\sqrt{x} - 3) = 25 - 4$

$3(2\sqrt{x} - 3) = 21$

Then carry out the operations for the parenthetical terms.

$3(2\sqrt{x} - 3) = 21$

$6\sqrt{x} - 9 = 21$

$6\sqrt{x} - 9 + 9 = 21 + 9$

$6\sqrt{x} = 30$

Then isolate $\sqrt{x}$.

$6\sqrt{x} \div 6 = 30 \div 6$

$\sqrt{x} = 5$

However, we are solving for x, not for $\sqrt{x}$.

So, we have to square each side of the equation in order to solve the problem.

$\sqrt{x} \times \sqrt{x} = 5 \times 5$

$x = 25$

21) The correct answer is B.

The Smith family is having lunch in a diner. They buy hot dogs and hamburgers to eat. The hot dogs cost $2.50 each, and the hamburgers cost $4 each. They buy 3 hamburgers. They also buy hot dogs. The total value of their purchase is $22. How many hot dogs did they buy?

Remember to assign variables to the items and then multiply each variable by its price.

The number of hot dogs is D and the number of hamburgers is H.

So, your equation is: $(D \times \$2.50) + (H \times \$4) = \$22$

The number of hamburgers is 3, so put that in the equation and solve it.

$(D \times \$2.50) + (H \times \$4) = \$22$

$(D \times \$2.50) + (3 \times \$4) = \$22$

$(D \times \$2.50) + 12 = \$22$

$(D \times \$2.50) + 12 - 12 = \$22 - 12$

$(D \times \$2.50) = \$10$

$\$2.50D = \$10$

$\$2.50D \div \$2.50 = \$10 \div \$2.50$

$D = 4$

22) The correct answer is D.

Simplify: $(x + 5) - (x^2 - 2x)$

First, remove the parentheses, paying attention to the negative sign in front of the second set of parentheses.

$(x + 5) - (x^2 - 2x) =$

$x + 5 - x^2 + 2x$

Now simplify for the common terms.

$x + 5 - x^2 + 2x =$

$x + 2x + 5 - x^2 =$

$x + 2x - x^2 + 5 =$

$3x - x^2 + 5$

23) The correct answer is D.

$(-3x^2 + 7x + 2) - (x^2 - 5) = ?$

Remove the negative sign in front of the second set of parentheses by performing the operations on the double negative.

$(-3x^2 + 7x + 2) - (x^2 - 5) =$

$(-3x^2 + 7x + 2) - x^2 + 5$

Then remove the first set of parentheses.

$(-3x^2 + 7x + 2) - x^2 + 5 =$

$-3x^2 + 7x + 2 - x^2 + 5$

Then group like terms together to solve the problem.

$-3x^2 + 7x + 2 - x^2 + 5 =$

$-3x^2 - x^2 + 7x + 2 + 5 =$

$-4x^2 + 7x + 7$

24) The correct answer is B.

115

$$\frac{x^2 + 10x + 16}{x^2 + 11x + 18} \times \frac{x^2 + 9x}{x^2 + 17x + 72} = ?$$

For this type of problem, first you need to find the factors of the numerators and denominators of each fraction.

As we have explained in the review section at the beginning of this book, when there are only addition signs in the rational expression, the factors will be in the following format:

(+)(+)

STEP 1: The numerator of the first fraction is $x^2 + 10x + 16$, so the final integer is 16.

The factors of 16 are:

1 × 16 = 16

2 × 8 = 16

4 × 4 = 16

Then add these factors together to discover what integer you need to use in front of the second term of the expression.

1 + 16 = 17

2 + 8 = 10

4 + 4 = 8

2 and 8 satisfy both parts of the equation.

Therefore, the factors of $x^2 + 10x + 16$ are $(x + 2)(x + 8)$.

Now factor the other parts of the problem.

STEP 2: The denominator of the first fraction is $x^2 + 11x + 18$, so the final integer is 18.

The factors of 18 are:

1 × 18 = 18

2 × 9 = 18

3 × 6 = 18

Add these factors together to find the integer to use in front of the second term of the expression.

1 + 18 = 19

2 + 9 = 11

3 + 6 = 9

Therefore, the factors of $x^2 + 11x + 18$ are $(x + 2)(x + 9)$.

STEP 3: The numerator of the second fraction is $x^2 + 9x$, so there is no final integer.

Because x is common to both terms of the expression, the factor will be in this format:

$x(x + \quad)$

Therefore, the factors of $x^2 + 9x$ are $x(x + 9)$.

STEP 4: The denominator of the second fraction is $x^2 + 17x + 72$, so the final integer is 72.

The factors of 72 are:

1 × 72 = 72

2 × 36 = 72

3 × 24 = 72

4 × 18 = 72

6 × 12 = 72

8 × 9 = 72

Add these factors together to find the integer to use in front of the second term of the expression.

1 + 72 = 73

2 + 36 = 38

3 + 24 = 27

4 + 18 = 22

6 + 12 = 18

8 + 9 = 17

Therefore, the factors of $x^2 + 17x + 72$ are $(x + 8)(x + 9)$.

Now we can solve our problem with the factors that we have found in each step.

$$\frac{x^2 + 10x + 16}{x^2 + 11x + 18} = \frac{(x+2)(x+8)}{(x+2)(x+9)} \qquad \frac{x^2 + 9x}{x^2 + 17x + 72} = \frac{x(x+9)}{(x+8)(x+9)}$$

So, replace the polynomials in the question with their factors from above.

$$\frac{x^2 + 10x + 16}{x^2 + 11x + 18} \times \frac{x^2 + 9x}{x^2 + 17x + 72} =$$

$$\frac{(x+2)(x+8)}{(x+2)(x+9)} \times \frac{x(x+9)}{(x+8)(x+9)}$$

Then for each fraction, you need to simplify by removing the common factors.

Remove $(x + 2)$ from the first fraction.

$$\frac{(x+2)(x+8)}{(x+2)(x+9)} \times \frac{x(x+9)}{(x+8)(x+9)} =$$

$$\frac{(x+8)}{(x+9)} \times \frac{x(x+9)}{(x+8)(x+9)}$$

Then remove $(x + 9)$ from the second fraction.

$$\frac{(x+8)}{(x+9)} \times \frac{x(x+9)}{(x+8)(x+9)} =$$

$$\frac{(x+8)}{(x+9)} \times \frac{x}{(x+8)}$$

Once you have simplified each fraction as above, perform the operation indicated. In this problem, you need to multiply the two fractions.

$$\frac{(x+8)}{(x+9)} \times \frac{x}{(x+8)} = \frac{x(x+8)}{(x+9)(x+8)}$$

When you have completed the operation, you need to check to see whether any further simplification is possible.

In this case, the fraction may be further simplified because the numerator and denominator share the common factor $(x + 8)$.

$$\frac{x(x+8)}{(x+9)(x+8)} = \frac{x}{x+9}$$

So, our final answer is $\dfrac{x}{x+9}$

25) The correct answer is C.

$\sqrt{5b-4} = 4$ What is the value of b?

In order to find the value of a variable inside a square root sign, your first step is to square each side of the equation.

$$\sqrt{(5b-4)^2} = 4^2$$

$$5b - 4 = 16$$

Then place the integers on one side of the equation.

$$5b - 4 = 16$$

$$5b - 4 + 4 = 16 + 4$$

$$5b = 20$$

Then isolate the variable to one side of the equation in order to solve the problem.

$$5b \div 5 = 20 \div 5$$

$$b = 4$$

26) The correct answer is D.

$$\frac{5z-5}{z} \div \frac{6z-6}{5z^2} = ?$$

When dividing fractions, you need to invert the second fraction and then multiply the two fractions together.

$$\frac{5z-5}{z} \div \frac{6z-6}{5z^2} =$$

$$\frac{5z-5}{z} \times \frac{5z^2}{6z-6}$$

When multiplying fractions, you multiply the numerator of the first fraction by the numerator of the second fraction and denominator of the first fraction by the denominator of the second fraction.

$$\frac{5z-5}{z} \times \frac{5z^2}{6z-6} =$$

$$\frac{5z^2(5z-5)}{z(6z-6)} =$$

$$\frac{25z^3 - 25z^2}{6z^2 - 6z}$$

Then look at the numerator and denominator from the result of the previous step to see if you can factor and simplify.

In this case, the numerator and denominator have the common factor of $(z^2 - z)$.

$$\frac{25z^3 - 25z^2}{6z^2 - 6z} =$$

$$\frac{25z(z^2 - z)}{6(z^2 - z)} =$$

$$\frac{25z}{6}$$

27) The correct answer is C.

If $c = \dfrac{a}{1-b}$, then b = ?

First you need to get rid of the fraction. To eliminate the fraction, multiply each side of the equation by the denominator of the fraction.

$$c = \frac{a}{1-b}$$

$$c \times (1-b) = \frac{a}{1-b} \times (1-b)$$

$$c \times (1-b) = a$$

Then simplify the side of the equation with the variable that you need to isolate, in this case b.

$$c \times (1-b) = a$$

$$c(1-b) \div c = a \div c$$

$$1 - b = \frac{a}{c}$$

Then isolate b by dealing with the integer and the negative sign in order to solve the problem.

$$1 - b = \frac{a}{c}$$

$$1 - 1 - b = \frac{a}{c} - 1$$

$$-b = \frac{a}{c} - 1$$

$$-b \times -1 = \left(\frac{a}{c} - 1\right) \times -1$$

$$b = -\frac{a}{c} + 1$$

28) The correct answer is C.

$$\sqrt{14x^5} \times \sqrt{6x^3} = ?$$

First do the multiplication of the integers. Remember that when there are exponents inside the square root signs, you add the exponents together.

So, multiply the integers and add the exponents.

$$\sqrt{14x^5} \times \sqrt{6x^3} = \sqrt{84x^8}$$

Then factor the integer inside the square root sign and simplify.

Remember that if you are finding factors for integers inside a radical, you should look for factors that have whole number square roots.

4 is the only factor of 84 that has a whole number as a square root because the square root of 4 is 2.

So, we factor as follows:

$$\sqrt{84x^8} = \sqrt{4 \times 21x^8}$$

Then we simplify like this:

$$\sqrt{4 \times 21x^8} =$$

$$\sqrt{(2 \times 2) \times 21x^8} =$$

$$2\sqrt{21x^8}$$

In order to simplify further, we need to deal with the x term.

Remember that the square root of any number is that number to the ½ power.

For example, $\sqrt{x} = x^{\frac{1}{2}}$

So, we can further simplify the x term in our problem.

$$2\sqrt{21x^8} =$$

$$2 \times \sqrt{21} \times x^{\frac{8}{2}}$$

$$2 \times \sqrt{21} \times x^4$$

$$2x^4\sqrt{21}$$

28) The correct answer is C.

$$\sqrt{14x^5} \times \sqrt{6x^3} = ?$$

First do the multiplication of the integers. Remember that when there are exponents inside the square root signs, you add the exponents together.

So, multiply the integers and add the exponents.

$$\sqrt{14x^5} \times \sqrt{6x^3} = \sqrt{84x^8}$$

Then factor the integer inside the square root sign and simplify.

Remember that if you are finding factors for integers inside a radical, you should look for factors that have whole number square roots.

4 is the only factor of 84 that has a whole number as a square root because the square root of 4 is 2.

So, we factor as follows:

$$\sqrt{84x^8} = \sqrt{4 \times 21x^8}$$

Then we simplify like this:

$$\sqrt{4 \times 21x^8} =$$

$$\sqrt{(2 \times 2) \times 21x^8} =$$

$$2\sqrt{21x^8}$$

In order to simplify further, we need to deal with the x term.

Remember that the square root of any number is that number to the ½ power.

For example, $\sqrt{x} = x^{\frac{1}{2}}$

So, we can further simplify the x term in our problem.

$$2\sqrt{21x^8} =$$

$$2 \times \sqrt{21} \times x^{\frac{8}{2}}$$

$$2 \times \sqrt{21} \times x^4$$

$$2x^4 \sqrt{21}$$

29) The correct answer is D.

$$8ab^2(3ab^4 + 2b) = ?$$

Remember to multiply the integers, but to add the exponents.

Also remember that any variable times itself is equal to that variable squared. For example, a × a = a^2

$$8ab^2(3ab^4 + 2b) =$$

$$(8ab^2 \times 3ab^4) + (8ab^2 \times 2b) =$$

$$24a^2b^6 + 16ab^3$$

30) The correct answer is D.

Perform the operation and express as one fraction: $\dfrac{5}{12x} + \dfrac{4}{10x^2} = ?$

First you have to find the lowest common denominator (LCD).

For denominators that have integers and variables, you need two steps in order to find the LCD.

(1) Deal with the integers in the denominator.

(2) Then deal with the variable.

In order to find the LCD, ask yourself: What is the smallest possible number that is divisible by both 12 and by 10? The answer is 60.

Alternatively, find the factors of 12 and 10, and then multiply by the factor that they do not have in common.

12 = 2 × 6 and 10 = 2 × 5, so multiply 12 by 5 and 10 by 6 to arrive at 60 for the integer part of the denominator.

Then deal with the variable. $x = x \times 1$ and $x^2 = x \times x$, so multiply $x^2 \times 1$ and $x \times x$, to get x^2 for the variable part of the denominator.

Then put together the product of the LCD for the integer and the product of the LCD for the variable.

60 for the integer

x^2 for the variable

So, the LCD is $60x^2$.

$$\frac{5}{12x} + \frac{4}{10x^2} =$$

$$\left(\frac{5}{12x} \times \frac{5x}{5x}\right) + \left(\frac{4}{10x^2} \times \frac{6}{6}\right) ==$$

$$\frac{25x}{60x^2} + \frac{24}{60x^2} =$$

$$\frac{25x + 24}{60x^2}$$

PERT Math Practice Test 3 – Answers:

1) The correct answer is A.

In the standard (x, y) plane, what is the distance between $(3\sqrt{3}, -1)$ and $(6\sqrt{3}, 2)$?

To solve problems asking for the distance between two points (x_1, y_1) and (x_2, y_2), you need to use the distance formula.

$$d = \sqrt{(x_2 - x_1)^2 + (y_2 - y_1)^2}$$

Now we need to put in the values stated: $(3\sqrt{3}, -1)$ and $(6\sqrt{3}, 2)$

$$d = \sqrt{(6\sqrt{3} - 3\sqrt{3})^2 + (2 - -1)^2}$$

$$d = \sqrt{(3\sqrt{3})^2 + (3)^2}$$

$$d = \sqrt{(9 \times 3) + 9}$$

$$d = \sqrt{27 + 9}$$

$$d = \sqrt{36}$$

$$d = 6$$

2) The correct answer is D.

Perform the operation: $\sqrt{5}(\sqrt{20} - \sqrt{5})$

Multiply the radical in front of the parentheses by each radical inside the parentheses.

$$\sqrt{5}(\sqrt{20} - \sqrt{5}) =$$

$$(\sqrt{5} \times \sqrt{20}) - (\sqrt{5} \times \sqrt{5}) =$$

$$\sqrt{100} - \sqrt{25}$$

Then find the square roots and subtract.

$$\sqrt{100} - \sqrt{25} =$$

$$\sqrt{10 \times 10} - \sqrt{5 \times 5} =$$

$$10 - 5 = 5$$

3) The correct answer is B.

$$8^7 \times 8^3 = ?$$

This question tests your knowledge of exponent laws.

First look to see whether your base number is the same on each part of the equation.

In this question, 8 is the base number for each part of the equation.

If the base number is the same, and the problem asks you to multiply, you simply add the exponents.

$$8^7 \times 8^3 =$$

$$8^{(7 + 3)} =$$

$$8^{10}$$

If the base number is the same, and the problem asks you to divide, you subtract the exponents.

4) The correct answer is A.

Solve by elimination:

$$x + 5y = 24$$

$$8x + 2y = 40$$

In order to solve by elimination, you need to subtract the second equation from the first equation.

Look at the term containing x in the second equation. We have $8x$ in the second equation.

In order to eliminate the term containing x, we need to multiply the first equation by 8.

$$x + 5y = 24$$

$$(8 \times x) + (5y \times 8) = (24 \times 8)$$

$8x + 40y = 192$

Now do the subtraction.

$$\begin{array}{r} 8x + 40y = 192 \\ -(8x + 2y = 40) \\ \hline 38y = 152 \end{array}$$

Then solve for y.

$38y = 152$

$38y \div 38 = 152 \div 38$

$y = 4$

Now put the value for *y* into the first equation and solve for *x*.

$x + 5y = 24$

$x + (5 \times 4) = 24$

$x + 20 = 24$

$x + 20 - 20 = 24 - 20$

$x = 4$

Therefore, $x = 4$ and $y = 4$, so the answer is (4, 4).

5) The correct answer is C.

Perform the operation: $(4x - 3)(5x^2 + 12x + 11) = ?$

For problems like this one, you need to multiply the first term in the first set of parentheses by all of the terms in the second set of parentheses.

Then multiply the second term in the first set of parentheses by all of the terms in the second set of parentheses.

So, you need to multiply as shown.

$(4x - 3)(5x^2 + 12x + 11) =$

$$[(4x \times 5x^2) + (4x \times 12x) + (4x \times 11)] - [(3 \times 5x^2) + (3 \times 12x) + (3 \times 11)] =$$

$$(20x^3 + 48x^2 + 44x) - (15x^2 + 36x + 33)$$

Then simplify, remembering to be careful about the negative sign in front of the second set of parentheses.

$$(20x^3 + 48x^2 + 44x) - (15x^2 + 36x + 33) =$$

$$(20x^3 + 48x^2 + 44x) - 15x^2 - 36x - 33 =$$

$$20x^3 + 48x^2 - 15x^2 + 44x - 36x - 33 =$$

$$20x^3 + 33x^2 + 8x - 33$$

6) The correct answer is C.

Remember to multiply the integers inside the two square root signs and add the exponents when multiplying the two terms.

$$\sqrt{6x^3}\sqrt{24x^5} =$$

$$\sqrt{144x^8}$$

Then find the square root, if possible.

$$\sqrt{144x^8} =$$

$$\sqrt{(12 \times 12)(x^4 \times x^4)} =$$

$$12x^4$$

7) The correct answer is B.

$$\sqrt{18} + 3\sqrt{32} + 5\sqrt{8} = ?$$

Factor the integers inside each of the square root signs.

Remember that you need to find a squared number for one of the factors for each radical.

$$\sqrt{18} + 3\sqrt{32} + 5\sqrt{8} =$$

$$\sqrt{2 \times 9} + 3\sqrt{2 \times 16} + 5\sqrt{2 \times 4} =$$

$$\sqrt{2 \times (3 \times 3)} + 3\sqrt{2 \times (4 \times 4)} + 5\sqrt{2 \times (2 \times 2)} =$$

$$3\sqrt{2} + (3 \times 4)\sqrt{2} + (5 \times 2)\sqrt{2}$$

Then do the multiplication and addition.

$$3\sqrt{2} + (3 \times 4)\sqrt{2} + (5 \times 2)\sqrt{2} =$$

$$3\sqrt{2} + 12\sqrt{2} + 10\sqrt{2} =$$

$$(3 + 12 + 10)\sqrt{2} =$$

$$25\sqrt{2}$$

8) The correct answer is D.

What equation represents the slope-intercept formula for the following data?

Through (4, 5); $m = -\dfrac{3}{5}$

You will remember that the slope intercept formula is: $y = mx + b$

Remember that m is the slope and b is the y intercept.

You will also need the slope formula: $m = \dfrac{y_2 - y_1}{x_2 - x_1}$

We are given the slope, as well as the point (4,5), so first we need to put those points into the slope formula.

We are doing this in order to solve for b, which is not provided in the facts of the problem.

$$\frac{y_2 - y_1}{x_2 - x_1} = -\frac{3}{5}$$

$$\frac{5 - y_1}{4 - x_1} = -\frac{3}{5}$$

Then eliminate the denominator.

$$\left(4-x_1\right)\frac{5-y_1}{4-x_1} = -\frac{3}{5}\left(4-x_1\right)$$

$$5-y_1 = -\frac{3}{5}\left(4-x_1\right)$$

Now put in 0 for x_1 in the slope formula in order to find b, which is the y intercept (the point at which the line crosses the y axis).

$$5-y_1 = -\frac{3}{5}\left(4-x_1\right)$$

$$5-y_1 = -\frac{3}{5}\left(4-0\right)$$

$$5-y_1 = -\frac{3\times 4}{5}$$

$$5-y_1 = -\frac{12}{5}$$

$$5-5-y_1 = -\frac{12}{5}-5$$

$$-y_1 = -\frac{12}{5}-5$$

$$-y_1 \times -1 = \left(-\frac{12}{5}-5\right)\times -1$$

$$y_1 = \frac{12}{5}+5$$

$$y_1 = \frac{12}{5}+\left(5\times \frac{5}{5}\right)$$

$$y_1 = \frac{12}{5}+\frac{25}{5}$$

$$y_1 = \frac{12 + 25}{5}$$

$$y_1 = \frac{37}{5}$$

Remember that the y intercept (known in the slope-intercept formula as the variable b) exists when x is equal to 0.

We have put in the value of 0 for x in the equation above, so $b = \dfrac{37}{5}$

Now put the value for b into the slope intercept formula.

$y = mx + b$

$$y = -\frac{3}{5}x + \frac{37}{5}$$

9) The correct answer is D.

For all $a \neq b$, $\dfrac{\dfrac{5a}{b}}{\dfrac{2a}{a-b}} = ?$

When you have fractions in the numerator and denominator of another fraction, you can divide the two fractions as follows:

$$\frac{\dfrac{5a}{b}}{\dfrac{2a}{a-b}} = \frac{5a}{b} \div \frac{2a}{a-b}$$

Then invert and multiply just like you would for any other fraction.

$$\frac{5a}{b} \div \frac{2a}{a-b} =$$

$$\frac{5a}{b} \times \frac{a-b}{2a} =$$

$$\frac{5a^2 - 5ab}{2ab}$$

Then simplify, if possible.

$$\frac{5a^2 - 5ab}{2ab} =$$

$$\frac{a(5a - 5b)}{a(2b)} =$$

$$\frac{5a - 5b}{2b}$$

10) The correct answer is D.

Perform the operation and express as one fraction: $\dfrac{1}{a+1} + \dfrac{1}{a}$

Find the lowest common denominator.

$$\frac{1}{a+1} + \frac{1}{a} =$$

$$\left(\frac{1}{a+1} \times \frac{a}{a}\right) + \left(\frac{1}{a} \times \frac{a+1}{a+1}\right) =$$

$$\frac{a}{a^2 + a} + \frac{a+1}{a^2 + a}$$

Then simplify, if possible

$$\frac{a}{a^2 + a} + \frac{a+1}{a^2 + a} =$$

$$\frac{a + a + 1}{a^2 + a} =$$

$$\frac{2a + 1}{a^2 + a}$$

11) The correct answer is B.

$$\frac{\sqrt{48}}{3} + \frac{5\sqrt{5}}{6} = ?$$

Find the lowest common denominator.

$$\frac{\sqrt{48}}{3} + \frac{5\sqrt{5}}{6} =$$

$$\left(\frac{\sqrt{48}}{3} \times \frac{2}{2}\right) + \frac{5\sqrt{5}}{6} =$$

$$\frac{2\sqrt{48}}{6} + \frac{5\sqrt{5}}{6}$$

Then simplify, if possible.

$$\frac{2\sqrt{48}}{6} + \frac{5\sqrt{5}}{6} =$$

$$\frac{2\sqrt{16 \times 3} + 5\sqrt{5}}{6} =$$

$$\frac{2\sqrt{(4 \times 4) \times 3} + 5\sqrt{5}}{6} =$$

$$\frac{(2 \times 4)\sqrt{3} + 5\sqrt{5}}{6} =$$

$$\frac{8\sqrt{3} + 5\sqrt{5}}{6}$$

12) The correct answer is D.

For all $x \neq 0$ and $y \neq 0$, $\dfrac{4x}{\frac{1}{xy}} = ?$

When the denominator of a fraction contains another fraction, treat the main fraction as the division sign.

$$\frac{4x}{\frac{1}{xy}} = 4x \div \frac{1}{xy}$$

Then invert and multiply as usual.

$$4x \div \frac{1}{xy} = 4x \times \frac{xy}{1}$$

$$4x \times \frac{xy}{1} = 4x \times xy$$

$$4x \times xy = 4x^2 y$$

13) The correct answer is C.

$$10a^2 b^3 c \div 2ab^2 c^2 = ?$$

First perform the division on the integers.

$$10 \div 2 = 5$$

Then do the division on the other variables.

$$a^2 \div a = a$$

$$b^3 \div b^2 = b$$

$$c \div c^2 = \frac{1}{c}$$

Then multiply these together to get the solution.

$$5 \times a \times b \times \frac{1}{c} =$$

$$\frac{5ab}{c} = 5ab \div c$$

14) The correct answer is D.

If x and y are positive integers, the expression $\dfrac{1}{\sqrt{x} - \sqrt{y}}$ is equivalent to what expression?

First of all, you have to eliminate the radicals in the denominator by factoring.

When you have two different variables in a rational expression such as x and y in this problem and your second variable is negative, your factored equation will be in the format $(\ +\ )(\ -\ )$.

We know that one sign will be positive and the other will be negative when we factor because we can get a negative product only when we multiply a positive number with a negative number. So, we will multiply the denominator as follows:

$$\left(\sqrt{x}+\sqrt{y}\right)\left(\sqrt{x}-\sqrt{y}\right)$$

We can swap the order of the sets of parentheses to make the multiplication a bit easier to follow.

$$\left(\sqrt{x}+\sqrt{y}\right)\left(\sqrt{x}-\sqrt{y}\right)=$$
$$\left(\sqrt{x}-\sqrt{y}\right)\left(\sqrt{x}+\sqrt{y}\right)$$

Now we are ready to solve the problem.

$$\frac{1}{\sqrt{x}-\sqrt{y}}=$$

$$\frac{1}{\sqrt{x}-\sqrt{y}}\times\frac{\sqrt{x}+\sqrt{y}}{\sqrt{x}+\sqrt{y}}$$

Simplify the numerator and multiply the radicals in the denominator by using the FOIL method.

$$\frac{1}{\sqrt{x}-\sqrt{y}}\times\frac{\sqrt{x}+\sqrt{y}}{\sqrt{x}+\sqrt{y}}=$$

$$\frac{\sqrt{x}+\sqrt{y}}{\sqrt{x}^{2}+\sqrt{xy}-\sqrt{xy}-\sqrt{y}^{2}}=$$

$$\frac{\sqrt{x}+\sqrt{y}}{\left(\sqrt{x}\right)^{2}-\left(\sqrt{y}\right)^{2}}$$

Then simplify the denominator.

$$\frac{\sqrt{x}+\sqrt{y}}{(\sqrt{x})^2-(\sqrt{y})^2}=$$

$$\frac{\sqrt{x}+\sqrt{y}}{x-y}$$

15) The correct answer is D.

$$(2+\sqrt{6})^2 = \ ?$$

Don't worry about the radical. This is just another type of FOIL problem.

$$(2+\sqrt{6})^2 =$$

$$(2+\sqrt{6})(2+\sqrt{6}) =$$

First . . . Outside . . Inside . . . Last

$$(2\times 2)+(2\times\sqrt{6})+(2\times\sqrt{6})+(\sqrt{6}\times\sqrt{6}) =$$

$$(2\times 2)+(2\sqrt{6}+2\sqrt{6})+\sqrt{6}^2 =$$

$$4+4\sqrt{6}+6 =$$

$$10+4\sqrt{6}$$

16) The correct answer is D.

$$\sqrt[3]{5}\times\sqrt[3]{7} = \ ?$$

Remember for problems like this, you need to multiply the amounts inside the square root sign, but leave the cube root as it is.

$$\sqrt[3]{5}\times\sqrt[3]{7} = \sqrt[3]{35}$$

17) The correct answer is B.

What is the value of $\dfrac{x-3}{2-x}$ when $x = 1$?

Substitute 1 for x.

$$\frac{x-3}{2-x} =$$

$$\frac{1-3}{2-1} =$$

$$(1-3) \div (2-1) =$$

$$-2 \div 1 =$$

$$-2$$

18) The correct answer is C.

The term PPM, pulses per minute, is used to determine how many heartbeats an individual has every 60 seconds. In order to calculate PPM, the pulse is taken for ten seconds, represented by variable P. What equation is used to calculate PPM?

Since there are 60 seconds in a minute, and pulse is measured in 10 second units, we divide the seconds as follows: $60 \div 10 = 6$

Accordingly, the PPM is calculated by talking P times 6: PPM = P6

19) The correct answer is D.

Medical authorities have recommended that an individual's ideal PPM is 60. What equation is used to calculate by how much a person's PPM exceeds the ideal PPM?

The PPM is calculated as in the previous problem.

In order to find the excess amount, we deduct the ideal PPM of 60 from the patient's actual PPM.

PPM − 60

20) The correct answer is A.

A runner of a 100 mile endurance race ran at a speed of 5 miles per hour for the first 80 miles of the race and x miles per hour for the last 20 miles of the race. What equation represents the runner's average speed for the entire race?

Miles per hour (MPH) is calculated as follows:

miles ÷ hours = MPH

So, if we have the MPH and the miles traveled, we need to change the above equation in order to calculate the hours.

miles ÷ hours = MPH

miles ÷ hours × hours = MPH × hours

miles = MPH × hours

miles ÷ MPH = (MPH × hours) ÷ MPH

miles ÷ MPH = hours

In other words, we divide the number of miles by the miles per hour to get the time for each part of the race.

So, for the first part of the race, the hours are calculated as follows:

80 ÷ 5

For the second part of the race, we take the remaining mileage and divide by the unknown variable.

20 ÷ x

Since the race is divided into two parts, these two results added together equal the total time.

Total time = [(80 ÷ 5) + (20 ÷ x)]

The total amount of miles for the race is then divided by the total time to get the average miles per hour for the entire race.

That is because MPH is calculated as follows:

MPH = miles ÷ hours

We have a 100 mile race, so the result is:

100 ÷ [(80 ÷ 5) + (20 ÷ x)]

21) The correct answer is D.

$3^4 \times 3^3 = ?$

Remember to add the exponents when multiplying.

$3^4 \times 3^3 = 3^{3+4} = 3^7$

22) The correct answer is D.

The number of bottles of soda that a soft drink factory can produce during D number of days using production method A is represented by the following equation:

$D^5 + 12,000$

Alternatively, the number of bottles of soda that can be produced using production method B is represented by this equation:

$D \times 10,000$

What is the largest number of bottles of soda that can be produced by the factory during a 10 day period?

First we have to calculate the output for our first production method.

For 10 days:

$D^5 + 12,000 =$

$10^5 + 12,000 =$

$100,000 + 12,000 =$

$112,000$

Then we have to calculate the output for the other production method.

$10 \times 10,000 = 100,000$

112,000 is greater than the 100,000 amount that method B yields.

So, the greatest amount of production for 10 days is 112,000 bottles.

23) The correct answer is C.

$5^8 \div 5^2 = ?$

If the base number is the same, and the problem asks you to divide, you subtract the exponents.

$$5^8 \div 5^2 = 5^{8-2} = 5^6$$

24) The correct answer is C.

The facts of our problem are as follows:

A driver travels at 60 miles per hour for two and a half hours before her car fails to start at a service station.

The driver has to wait two hours while the car is repaired before she can continue driving.

She then drives at 75 miles an hour for the remainder of her journey.

She is traveling to Denver, and her journey is 240 miles in total.

If she left home at 6:00 am, what time will she arrive in Denver?

So, calculate the time for each part of the problem.

Time spent before needing the repair: 2.5 hours

Time spent waiting for the repair: 2 hours

Then we have to calculate the remaining time spent traveling to Denver.

We know that she traveled 150 miles before the repair.

Miles traveled before needing the repair: 60 MPH × 2.5 hours = 150 miles traveled

If the journey is 240 miles in total, she has 90 miles remaining after the car is repaired.

240 − 150 = 90

If she then travels at 75 miles an hour for 90 miles, the time she spends is:

90 ÷ 75 = 1.2 hours

Be careful with the decimal point!

There are 60 minutes in an hour, so 1.2 hours is 1 hour and 12 minutes because 60 minutes × 0.20 = 12 minutes.

The time spent traveling after the repair is 1 hour and 12 minutes.

Now add together all of the times to get your answer.

Time spent before needing the repair: 2.5 hours = 2 hours and 30 minutes

Time spent waiting for the repair: 2 hours

The time spent traveling after the repair: 1 hour and 12 minutes.

Total time: 5 hours and 42 minutes

If she left home at 6:00 am, she will arrive in Denver at 11:42 am.

25) The correct answer is B.

Which one of the following is a solution to the following ordered pairs of equations?

$y = -2x - 1$

$y = x - 4$

A) (0, 1)

B) (1, –3)

C) (4, 0)

D) (1, 3)

Plug in values for x and y to see if they work for both equations.

Answer choice (B) is the only answer that works for both equations.

If $x = 1$

then for $y = (-2 \times 1) - 1$

$y = -2 - 1$

$y = -3$

For the second equation:

$y = x - 4$

$-3 = x - 4$

$-3 + 4 = x - 4 + 4$

$-3 + 4 = x$

$1 = x$

26) The correct answer is A.

You need to create an equation to set out the facts of this problem. Here we will say that the total number of students is variable S.

$15 = (S - \frac{1}{4}S) \times \frac{1}{2}$

$15 = \frac{3}{4}S \times \frac{1}{2}$

$15 = \frac{3}{8}S$

$15 \times 8 = \frac{3}{8}S \times 8$

$120 = 3S$

$S = 40$

27) The correct answer is D.

Final Score = A + B + C

B = 2A

C = 3B = 3 × 2A = 6A

Now express the original equation in terms of A:

A + B + C = A + 2A + 6A = 9A

28) The correct answer is A.

For questions on systems of equations like this one, you should look at the multiplication equation first. Ask yourself, what are the factors of 24?

We know that 24 is the product of the following:

$1 \times 24 = 24$

$2 \times 12 = 24$

$3 \times 8 = 24$

$4 \times 6 = 24$

Now add each of the two factors together to solve the first equation.

1 + 24 = 25

2 + 12 = 14

3 + 8 = 11

4 + 6 = 10

(3, 8) solves both equations. Therefore, it is the correct answer.

29) The correct answer is C.

Our question stated that for all positive integers x and y: $x - 6 < 0$ and $y < x + 12$

$y < ?$

To solve inequalities like this one, you should first solve the equation for x.

$x - < 0$

$x - 6 + 6 < 0 + 6$

$x < 6$

Now solve for y by replacing x with its value.

$y < x + 12$

$y < 6 + 12$

$y < 18$

30) The correct answer is B.

Our problem asked for the solution of $2 + y < -8$

Isolate y in order to solve the problem.

$2 + y < -8$

$2 - 2 + y < -8 - 2$

$y < -10$

100 ADDITIONAL MATH EXERCISES WITH TIPS

Instructions: Complete the math questions that follow by selecting the correct answer from the options provided. You should read the tip following each question before choosing your answer. The answers and solutions are provided after the last exercise. You may wish to view the "Math Formula Sheet" at the end of the book for some of the questions.

Applying Standard Concepts

1) A company sells electronics online. The annual sales for the first three years of business were: $25,135, $32,787, and $47,004. What were the total sales for the past three years?
    A) $101,326   B) $104,916   C) $104,926   D) $104,944

> This is a question on adding whole numbers. The problem is asking for the total for all three years, so add the three figures together.

2) A customer gives the cashier $50 to pay for the items he purchased, which total $41.28. How much change should be given to the customer?
    A) $7.82   B) $8.18   C) $8.27   D) $8.72

> This is a question on subtracting whole numbers. To calculate the change, you need to take the amount of money the customer gives the cashier and subtract the amount of the purchase.

3) A car salesperson earns a $175 referral fee on every customer who accepts a customer service upgrade. The salesperson referred 8 customers for the service upgrade this month. How much did the salesperson earn in referral fees for the month?
    A) $1050   B) $1200   C) $1225   D) $1400

> This is a question on multiplying whole numbers. Multiplication problems will often include the words 'each' or 'every.' Multiply the amount of the referral fee by the number of customers to solve.

4) An employee's weekly pay is $535.50 and she works 30 hours per week. How much is she paid per hour?
    A) $17.83   B) $17.84   C) $17.85   D) $18.34

> This is a question on dividing whole numbers. Division problems will often include the word 'per.' Divide the total weekly amount by the number of hours to solve.

5) Business losses are represented as negative numbers, while business profits are represented as positive numbers. A business makes the following profits and losses during a four week period: –$286, $953, $1502, and –$107. What was the total business profit or loss during these four weeks?
    A) $2,026   B) $2,062   C) $2,080   D) –$2,026

> This is a question on adding negative numbers. When you have to add a negative number to a positive number, you are subtracting. So, add the business profits and subtract the business losses to solve.

6) Location below sea level is represented as a negative number. The location below sea level of Lake Alto is –35 meters. The location below sea level of Lake Bajo is 62 meters deeper than Lake Alto. What figure represents the location below sea level for Lake Bajo?

A) –97   B) 97   C) –62   D) –27

This is a question on subtracting negative numbers. The facts state that the location below sea level of Lake Bajo is 62 meters deeper than Lake Alto, so we need to subtract this figure from the location below sea level of Lake Alto. The location below sea level of Lake Alto is a negative number, so you are subtracting a negative from a negative.

7) A company has completed 3/5 of a project. What figure below expresses the project completion amount as a decimal number?

A) 0.06   B) 0.60   C) 1.67   D) 3.00

This is a question on changing fractions to decimals. To express a fraction as a decimal, treat the line in the fraction as the division symbol and divide accordingly. Remember to be careful with the decimal placement in your final answer.

8) A teacher reports attendance as a decimal figure, calculated as the number of students attending divided into the total number of students in the class. This week, the attendance was 0.55. What percentage best represents the attendance for this week?

A) 0.55%   B) 5.50%   C) 55.0%   D) 55.5%

This is a question on changing decimals to percentages. To express a decimal number as a percentage, move the decimal point two places to the right. Then add the percent sign.

9) An employee has used up 5/14 of his vacation days. Approximately what percentage of vacation days has the employee already used?

A) 0.357%   B) 2.800%   C) 3.571%   D) 35.7%

This is a question on changing fractions to decimals. Treat the line in the fraction as the division symbol and divide. Then move the decimal point two places to the right, and add the percent sign.

10) A driver has used 0.75 of the gas he last put in his car. What fraction best represents the amount of gas used?

A) 1/4   B) 2/5   C) 3/5   D) 3/4

This is a question on changing a decimal number to a fraction. You should be able to recognize the equivalent decimal numbers for commonly-used fractions such as ½ or ¾ for your exam. If you are unsure, perform division on the answer choices to solve.

11) It is reported that 33% of all new stores close within five years of opening. What fraction best represents this percentage?

A) 1/3   B) 1/4   C) 1/5   D) 2/3

This is a question on changing a percentage to a fraction. You should be able to recognize the equivalent fractions for commonly-used percentages for the test. If you are unsure of the answer, perform division on the answer choices to solve.

12) A carpet store is offering 45% off in a sale this month. What decimal number below best represents the percentage off?

A) 0.0045   B) 0.0450   C) 0.4500   D) 4.5000

This is a question on changing percentages to decimals. Any given percentage is out of 100%, so we divide by 100 to express a percentage as a decimal. So, move the decimal point two places to the left and remove the percent sign.

13) A bakery has to pay 36 cents for each pound of flour it buys. It decides to buy $14\frac{1}{4}$ pounds of flour today. How much will it have to pay?

A) $3.60   B) $5.13   C) $5.31   D) $142.50

This is a question on calculations involving units of money. Express both amounts as decimal numbers and multiply to solve.

14) A bookkeeper has just been with a client for 0.35 hours. Approximately how many minutes did the bookkeeper spend with this client?

A) 3.5 minutes   B) 5.8 minutes   C) 21 minutes   D) 35 minutes

This is a question on calculations involving units of time. There are 60 minutes in an hour, so multiply the minutes in the hour by the decimal number given in the problem to solve.

15) A flower store charges $24 for a small arrangement of flowers. A customer will get a $5 discount if he or she provides his or her own vase for the small arrangement. This month, there were 12 customers who ordered small arrangements and provided their own vases. How much money in total did the flower store make on arrangements sold to these 12 customers?

A) $228   B) $282   C) $288   D) $348

This is a question with two operations. Subtract the discount from the original price. Then multiply this figure by the number of units sold.

16) A bricklayer works for a construction company. He laid bricks for 7 hours per day for 4 days on one job. The customer was billed $45 per hour for his work, and he was paid $25 per hour. After the bricklayer's wages have been paid, how much money did the company make for his work on this job?

A) $175   B) $180   C) $315   D) $560

This question has three operations. First, you need to determine the total number of hours worked for the 4 days. Then calculate the profit the company makes per hour. Finally, multiply the total number of hours worked by the profit per hour to solve.

17) A pharmacist owns a local drug store. Last week, she filled 250 prescriptions in 40 hours. Assuming that each prescription takes the same amount of time, how many minutes should it take her to fill a single prescription?

A) 9.6 minutes   B) 6.25 minutes   C) 3.75 minutes   D) 0.16 minutes

This is a question with two operations. Since there are 60 minutes in an hour, we multiply by 60 to get the number of minutes. Then divide by the number of prescriptions to get the rate.

18) A truck driver delivered 120 orders this week. She delivered 105 of the orders on time. What percentage of the driver's orders was delivered on time?

A) 0.875%   B) 8.75%   C) 87.5%   D) 0.125%

This is a question with two operations. Take the amount of orders that were delivered on time and divide by the amount of total orders. Then convert to a percentage.

19) A scientist measures cell growth or attrition. Each day a measurement is taken. Cell growth is represented as a positive figure, while cell attrition is represented as a negative figure. On Monday cell growth was 27, and for all days Tuesday through Friday, cell attrition was 13 per day. What number represents total cell growth or attrition for these five days?

A) 25   B) –25   C) 40   D) –40

This is a question on multiplying negative numbers. Cell attrition is a negative number, so perform multiplication to get the total for Tuesday through Friday. Then add the cell growth for Monday to solve.

20) A vegetable farmer works until noon each day. The chart below shows the amounts of cucumbers per hour that she picked one morning:

7:00 to 8:00	23 cucumbers	10:00 to 11:00	24 cucumbers
8:00 to 9:00	25 cucumbers	11:00 to 12:00	22 cucumbers
9:00 to 10:00	26 cucumbers		

On average, how many cucumbers did the farmer pick per hour?

A) 23   B) 24   C) 25   D) 26

This is a question on calculating averages. The average is sometimes called the arithmetic mean, so you may see both terms on the test. To find the average, you need to add all of the amounts to get the total, and then divide the total by the number of hours.

21) A local company makes one particular kind of concrete. For this concrete, 2 units of sand have to be added to every 3 units of cement powder used. A batch of this concrete that has 66 units of cement powder is being made. How many units of sand should be added to this batch?

A) 2   B) 3   C) 22   D) 44

This is a question on a simple ratio. Take the 66 units of cement powder for the current batch and divide by the 3 units stated in the original ratio. Then multiply this result by the 2 units of sand stated in the original ratio to solve.

22) It is company policy that the ratio of employees to supervisors should be 50:1. So, for every 50 employees in a company, there should be 1 supervisor. If there are 255 employees, how many supervisors are there?

A) 1   B) 2   C) 3   D) 5

This is another question on a simple ratio. The problem states that we are working with a ratio, so the employees and the supervisors form separate groups. First, add the two groups together. Then take the total amount of employees stated in the problem and divide this by the figure you have just calculated to get the amount of supervisors.

23) A report shows that 2 out of every 20 employees in a particular company are interested in applying for a promotion. If the company has 480 employees in total, how many employees are interested in applying for a promotion?

A) 20   B) 24   C) 42   D) 48

This is a question on a simple proportion. Problems on proportions often use the phrase 'out of.' The problem uses the phrase '2 out of every 20 employees' so we know that there are 2 employees who form a subset within each group of 20. So, take the total number of employees and divide this by 20. Then multiply this result by the amount in the subset to solve.

24) A mechanic spent from 8:10 to 8:22 changing three wheel covers on a car. At this rate, how many wheel covers could he change per hour?

A) 3   B) 5   C) 15   D) 20

This is a question on calculating a simple rate. Calculate the amount of time in minutes that was spent on the three wheel covers. Then calculate the time in minutes needed to change 1 wheel cover. Then divide this amount into 60 minutes to solve.

25) A fencing company put up $15^2/_8$ yards of fence for one customer and $13^5/_8$ yards of fence for another customer. How many yards of fence did the company put up for both customers in total?

A) $28^3/_8$ B) $28^5/_8$ C) $28^7/_8$ D) $28^7/_{16}$

This is a question on adding fractions that have a common denominator. First, add the whole numbers that are in front of each fraction. Then add the fractions. If you have two fractions that have the same denominator, which is the number on the bottom of the fraction, you add the numerators and keep the common denominator. Then combine the new whole number and the new fraction to solve.

26) A food company fills gourmet food boxes with various products. So far today, $2^3/_8$ boxes have been filled for one order and $4^1/_8$ boxes have been filled for another order. How many total boxes have been filled so far today?

A) $6^1/_2$ B) $6^1/_4$ C) $6^3/_4$ D) $6^3/_{16}$

This is another question on adding fractions that have a common denominator. Follow the same steps as for the previous question, but also simplify the fraction to solve. This means that you have to reduce the numerator and denominator by dividing them by the same number, which is known as a common factor.

27) A customer has just placed an order to have an awning made for his front window. According to the measurements, $5^3/_{16}$ yards of canvas will be needed to make the awning. However, the customer calls later to say that his initial measurement was incorrect, and only $4^1/_{16}$ yards of canvas is actually needed to make the awning. Which fraction below represents the amount by which the amount of canvas has been reduced?

A) $1^1/_8$ B) $1^1/_{16}$ C) $1^1/_{32}$ D) $1^3/_{16}$

This is a question on subtracting fractions with a common denominator. First, subtract the whole numbers, and then subtract the fractions. If you have two fractions that have the same denominator, you subtract the numerators and keep the common denominator. Then simplify the fraction. Finally, combine the whole number and the simplified fraction to solve.

28) Certain additives need to be placed in a bottle to make a particular product. The company measures each additive in decimal units, with 1 unit representing the filled bottle. The bottle contains 0.25 units of additive A, 0.50 units of additive B, and 0.10 units of additive C. Which of the following represents, in terms of units, how full the bottle currently is?

A) 08.5 B) 0.85 C) 0.90 D) 0.95

This is a question on adding commonly-known decimals. Add the three figures together to solve. Remember to be sure to put the decimal point in the correct place when you work out the solution.

29) A recent survey shows that 50% of your customers rated your service as excellent and 25% rated your service as very good. What percentage below represents the total amount of customers who rated your service either excellent or very good?

A) 25% B) 50% C) 75% D) 85%

This is a question on adding commonly-known percentages. Simply add the percentages together to solve.

30) A customer has just ordered 5 units of a product. Each unit of the product takes $1^1/_4$ hours to make. How much time is needed to make this order?

A) 5 hours and 25 minutes C) 6 hours and 4 minutes
B) 5 hours and 55 minutes D) 6 hours and 15 minutes

This is a question on multiplying a mixed number by a whole number of units. First, multiply the whole numbers. Then multiply the whole number of units by the fraction. Then convert this improper fraction to a mixed number. Add the whole number and the mixed number, and convert to hours and minutes to solve.

31) A dressmaker who works in a tailoring shop is trying to decide what setting to use on the sewing machine. She has tried the 1/8 inch stitch but has realized that it is too small. The stitches on the machine are sized in 1/32 increments. What size stitch should she try next?

A) 3/16 B) 5/32 C) 6/16 D) 6/32

This is a question on performing calculations on fractions with different denominators. Convert 1/8 to the following equivalent fraction: 1/8 = ?/32

32) Amal runs a souvenir store that sells key rings. She can get 50 key rings from her first supplier for 50 cents each. She can get the same 50 keys rings from her second supplier for $30 in total or from her third supplier for $27.50. How much will she pay if she gets the best deal?
A) $25.00   B) $25.25   C) $25.50   D) $27.50

This is a question on finding the best deal when you have to perform a one-step calculation. Read the facts carefully, work out the total prices for all three suppliers, and then compare prices.

33) A budget hotel charges $45 per night and $280 per week. If a guest stays at the hotel for 9 nights, what is the least that he will pay for his stay?
A) $280   B) $315   C) $325   D) $370

This is a question on finding the best deal when you have to perform two-step calculations. Determine the duration of the stay in weeks and nights. Then add the cost for 1 week to the cost for 2 days to solve.

34) The price of an item is normally $15, but customers with a loyalty card can purchase it at the discounted price of $12. What percentage best represents the discount awarded to these customers?
A) 3%   B) 5%   C) 15%   D) 20%

This is a question on calculating the percentage of a discount. Divide the dollar amount of the discount by the original price to get the percentage of the discount.

35) A retail ceramics store sells mugs and bowls. It buys one type of mug for $3 and sells it for $9. It uses the same percentage mark up on one type of bowl that it buys for $4. What figure below represents the sales price of the bowl?
A) $6   B) $8   C) $12   D) $16

This is a question on calculating a markup. You need to calculate the percentage for the markup on the first product and apply this percentage markup to the second product. Remember to use the percentage markup, rather than a dollar value. You may need the following formulas if you don't already know how to calculate markup: Dollar value of markup = Sales price in dollars – Cost in dollars; Percentage markup = Dollar value of markup ÷ Cost in dollars

36) A company got $20 off of an order. This amounted to a 25% discount off the order. What would the company have paid without the discount?
A) $4   B) $5   C) $25   D) $80

This is a question on calculating a reverse percentage. To calculate a reverse percentage you need to divide, rather than multiply. So, take the dollar value of the discount and divide by the percentage to solve.

37) A company that fabricates cleaning products begins to make the first batch of products on Monday at 10:30 am. The actual production time is 3 hours and 25 minutes. This is followed by a bottling and labeling process that takes 1 hour and 40 minutes and a packaging process that takes a further 26 hours. If production keeps to this schedule, when will the first batch be ready for shipment?

A) Tuesday at 12:30 pm   C) Tuesday at 5:35 pm
B) Tuesday at 3:55 pm   D) Wednesday at 3:55 pm

This is a question on calculating the hours and minutes that have passed since the start of a job or process. Calculate the total time for the entire process and add to the starting time to solve.

38) Maria sells soft drinks in a convenience store that she runs. She can buy 240 soft drinks from one supplier for 25 cents each or from a different supplier for $58 for all 240 drinks. Both suppliers are in the same state, so she has to pay a sales tax of 6.5% on either purchase. If she chooses the best price for the soft drinks, including tax, how much will she pay in total?

A) $58.00   B) $60.00   C) $61.77   D) $63.90

This is an advanced question on finding the best deal. Remember to add the dollar amount of the sales tax to both calculations for this problem.

39) A picture framing store can make 20 small frames in 4 days or 21 large frames in 3 days. A customer has just placed an order with for 40 small frames and 64 large ones. Approximately how many days will it take to make them all?

A) 7   B) 11   C) 14   D) 17

This is a question on calculating production rates by unit. Determine the unit rates per day for each of the products by dividing the output by the number of days. Then divide the rates into the amount of items ordered to solve.

40) The report on a production order shows that 12.5% of the work has been completed in the past 4 days. If work continues at the same rate, how many more days will be required in order to finish the order?

A) 3   B) 4   C) 28   D) 32

This is a question on calculating rate by time. Calculate the percentage of work completed per day, and then determine how many days are needed for the job.

41) A physical therapist measures how far her clients are able to walk during each session. One client walked 123 feet and 6 inches during his first session and 138 feet and 8 inches during his second session. What is the combined total of the distance walked for the two sessions?

A) 261 feet 24 inches   C) 262 feet 8 inches
B) 261 feet 6 inches   D) 262 feet 2 inches

This is a question on performing a calculation with mixed units. It is usually easiest to perform one calculation with the feet and another with the inches. You may need to convert the total inches back to feet and inches if there are more than 12 inches in the second calculation.

42)   A nutritionist advises clients and sells supplements to them. A box containing the supplements weighs 8 pounds and 5 ounces when full. The box itself weighs 7 ounces when it is empty. Each supplement weighs 0.75 ounces. About how many supplements should be in the box?
    A) 168   B) 177   C) 178   D) 186

This is a question on performing conversions within systems of measurement. Here we have to convert between pounds and ounces. Convert the total weight of the product (excluding the box weight) to ounces then divide the total ounces by the ounces per unit to solve. 1 pound = 16 ounces

43)   It is company policy to have at least 60 yards of dark black yarn in stock at the start of every month. Inventory has been taken this morning and there are 2 balls of dark black yarn that are 75 inches each and 4 balls of dark black yarn that are $25^{1/4}$ inches each in stock. This yarn must be purchased in 5-yard-long balls. How many balls of yarn should be purchased in order to replenish the stock?
    A) 10   B) 11   C) 33   D) 36

This is a question on working with fractional units. Calculate the amount of remaining stock in inches, and then convert from inches to yards. Then calculate the amount required to restock. Remember that it is not possible to buy a fractional part of a ball, so you have to round up to solve.

Coordinate Geometry

44)   Find the midpoint of the line segment that connects the points (5, 2) and (7, 4).

    A) (6, 3)   B) (3, 6)   C) (3.5, 5.5)   D) (12, 6

45)   If store A is represented by the coordinates (−4, 2) and store B is represented by the coordinates (8,−6), and store A and store B are connected by a line segment, what is the midpoint of this line?

    A) (2, 2)   B) (2, −2)   C) (−2, 2)   D) (−2, −2)

The midpoint of two points on a two-dimensional graph is calculated by using the midpoint formula:

$$(x_1 + x_2) \div 2 , (y_1 + y_2) \div 2$$

46)   What is the distance between (2, 3) and (6, 7)?
    A)   4   B)   16   C) $\sqrt{16}$ D) $\sqrt{32}$

The distance formula is used to calculate the linear distance between two points on a two-dimensional graph. The two points are represented by the coordinates (x_1, y_1) and (x_2, y_2).
$$d = \sqrt{(x_2 - x_1)^2 + (y_2 - y_1)^2}$$

47)   The measurements of a mountain can be placed on a two-dimensional linear graph on which
        $x = 5$ and $y = 315$. If the line crosses the y axis at 15, what is the slope of this mountain?

        A) 60   B) 63   C) 300   D) 315

The slope formula: $m = \dfrac{y_2 - y_1}{x_2 - x_1}$

The slope-intercept formula: $y = mx + b$, where m is the slope and b is the y intercept.

Now use these formulas to solve the graph problem that follows.

48) Which of the following statements is true with respect to the lined graph below?

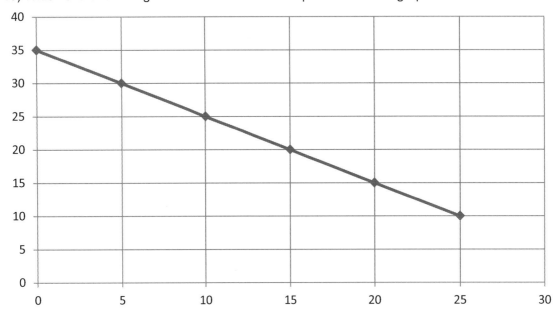

        A) The line has a slope of –1 and contains point (20, 15).
        B) The line has a slope of 1 and contains point (20, 15).
        C) The line has a slope of –1 and contains point (15, 20).
        D) The line has a slope of 1 and contains point (15, 20).

49)   State the x and y intercepts that fall on the straight line represented by the equation:
        $y = x + 14$
        A) (–14, 0) and (0, 14)   C) (14, 0) and (0, –14)
        B) (0, 14) and (0, –14)   D) (0, –14) and (14, 0)

50)   Find the x and y intercepts of the following equation: $x^2 + 2y^2 = 144$
        A) (12, 0) and (0, $\sqrt{72}$)   C) (0, $\sqrt{72}$) and (0, 12)
        B) (0, 12) and ($\sqrt{72}$, 0)   D) (12, 0) and ($\sqrt{72}$, 0)

For questions like the two above on x and y intercepts, substitute 0 for y in the equation provided to find
the value of x. Then substitute 0 for x to find the value of y and solve the problem.

Algebra

Expressions with One Variable

51) Evaluate: $2x^2 - x + 5$ if $x = -2$
   A) 2   B) 7   C) 15   D) 17

> Step 1 – To perform the operations on the first term of the equation, multiply –2 by itself to square it. Then multiply this result by 2. Step 2 – To get your final answer, take the result from step 1 and subtract –2 and add 5.

52) Solve for x: $-6x + 5 = -19$
   A) 2   B) 4   C) 6   D) 8

> Isolate x to one side of the equation by subtracting 5 from both sides of the equation. Then multiply each side of the new equation by –6 to isolate x and solve.

53) If $4x - 3(x + 2) = -3$, then $x = $?
   A) 9   B) 3   C) 1   D) –3

> Multiply the terms inside the parentheses by the –3 in front of the set of parentheses. Then simplify and isolate x to one side of the equation to solve.

54) If $\frac{3}{4}x - 2 = 4$, $x = $?
   A) $\frac{8}{3}$ B) $\frac{1}{8}$ C) 8   D) –8

> Multiply each side of the equation by $\frac{4}{3}$ to get rid of the fraction. Then simplify the remaining new improper fraction and add the result of the simplified fraction to both sides of the equation solve.

55) What is the value of $\frac{x-3}{2-x}$ when $x = 1$?

   A) 2   B) –2   C) $^1/_2$ D) $-^1/_2$

> Substitute 1 for the value of x. Then perform the subtraction in the numerator and the subtraction in the dominator. Then simplify the resulting fraction to solve.

Expressions with Two Variables

56) $x^2 + xy - y = 41$ and $x = 5$. What is the value of y?
   A) 2.6   B) 4   C) 6   D) –4

57) $x^2 + xy - y = 254$ and $x = 12$. What is the value of y?
   A) 110   B) 10   C) 11   D) 12

> For the two previous questions, substitute the stated values of x. Then perform the necessary operations on both sides of the equation to isolate y and solve.

Roots and Radicals

58) If 6 + 8(2√x + 4) = 62, then √x = ?

  A) 3.25   B) 24   C) $\frac{3}{2}$ D) $\frac{2}{3}$

Perform the multiplication on the parenthetical first. The get rid of the integers by subtracting them from both sides of the equations. Then divide by 16 to isolate √x to solve.

59) Which of the answers below is equal to the following radical expression? $\sqrt{50}$

  A) 1 ÷ 50   B) $2\sqrt{25}$ C) $2\sqrt{5}$ D) $5\sqrt{2}$

Step 1 – Factor the number inside the square root sign. Step 2 – Look to see if any of the factors are perfect squares. In this case, the only factor that is a perfect square is 25. Step 3 – Find the square root of 25 then simplify.

60) $\sqrt{36} + 4\sqrt{72} - 2\sqrt{144} = ?$

  A) $2\sqrt{36}$ B) $2\sqrt{252}$ C) $18 + 24\sqrt{2}$ D) $-18 + 24\sqrt{2}$

Step 1 – Find the common factors that are perfect squares. Step 2 – Factor the amounts inside each of the radical signs and simplify.

61) $\sqrt{7} \times \sqrt{11} = ?$

  A) $\sqrt{77}$ B) $\sqrt{18}$ C) $7\sqrt{11}$ D) $11\sqrt{7}$

Step 1 – Multiply the numbers inside the radical signs. Step 2 – Put this product inside a radical symbol for your answer.

62) Simplify: $\sqrt{15} + 3\sqrt{15}$

  A) 45   B) $4\sqrt{15}$ C) $2\sqrt{15}$ D) $3\sqrt{30}$

You can place the number 1 in front of the first radical because it will count only one time. Then add the numbers in front of the radical signs to solve.

63) Express as a rational number: $\sqrt[3]{\dfrac{216}{27}}$

  A) 3   B) 2   C) $\frac{7}{3}$ D) $\sqrt[3]{2}$

Step 1 – Find the cube roots of the numerator and denominator to eliminate the radical. Step 2 – Simplify further if possible. The cube root is a number that equals the required product when multiplied by itself two times.

Exponent Laws

64) $7^5 \times 7^3 = ?$

   A) 7^8 B) 7^{15} C) 14^8 D) 49^8

If the base number is the same, you need to add the exponents when multiplying, but keep the base number the same as before.

65) $xy^6 \div xy^3 = ?$

   A) xy^{18} B) xy^3 C) x^2y^3 D) xy^2

If the base number is the same, you need to subtract the exponents when dividing, but keep the base number the same as before.

66) $\sqrt{8x^4} \cdot \sqrt{32x^6} = ?$

   A) $8\sqrt{32x^{10}}$ B) $16x^{10}$ C) $16x^5$ D) $256x^{10}$

This question combines the laws or radicals with the laws of exponents.

67)   A rocket flies at a speed of 1.7×10^5 miles per hour for 2×10^{-1} hours. How far has this rocket gone?

   A) 340,000 miles   B) 34,000 miles   C) 3,400 miles   D) 340 miles

Step 1: Add the exponents to multiply the 10's. Step 2: Multiply the miles per hour by the number of hours to get the distance traveled. Step 3: Then multiply these two results together to solve the problem.

68) $\sqrt{x^{\frac{5}{7}}} = ?$

   A) $\dfrac{5x}{7}$ B) $\left(\sqrt[5]{x}\right)^7$ C) $\left(7\sqrt{x}\right)^5$ D) $\left(\sqrt[7]{x}\right)^5$

Step 1: Put the base number inside the radical sign. Step 2: The denominator of the exponent is the nth root of the radical. Step 3: The numerator is the new exponent.

69) $x^{-5} = ?$

   A) $\dfrac{1}{x^{-5}}$ B) $\dfrac{1}{x^5}$ C) –5x   D) $\dfrac{1}{5x}$

70) $(-4)^{-3} = ?$

A) -64 　　　　B) $-\frac{1}{64}$ 　　　　C) $\frac{1}{64}$ 　　　　D) 64

Step 1: When you have an exponent that is a negative number, you need to set up a fraction, where 1 is the numerator. Step 2: Put the term with the exponent in the denominator, but remove the negative sign on the exponent.

71) $62^0 = ?$

A) -62 　　　　B) 0 　　　　C) 1 　　　　D) 62

72) $(25x)^0 = ?$

A) 0 　　　　B) 5 　　　　C) 1 　　　　D) 25

Any non-zero number raised to the power of zero is equal to 1.

Simplifying Rational Algebraic Expressions

73) $\dfrac{b + \frac{2}{7}}{\frac{1}{b}} = ?$

A) $b^2 + \frac{7}{2}$ 　　　　B) $2b + \frac{7}{2}$ 　　　　C) $b^2 + \frac{2b}{7}$ 　　　　D) $\dfrac{b}{b + \frac{2}{7}}$

Step 1 – When the expression has fractions in both the numerator and denominator, treat the line in the main fraction as the division symbol. Step 2 – Invert the fraction that was in the denominator and multiply.

74) $\dfrac{x^2}{x^2 + 2x} + \dfrac{8}{x} = ?$

A) $\dfrac{x + 8x + 16}{x^2 + 2x}$ 　　　　B) $\dfrac{x^2 + 8}{x^2 + 3x}$ 　　　　C) $\dfrac{8x^2 + 16x}{x^3}$ 　　　　D) $\dfrac{x^2 + 8x + 16}{x^2 + 2x}$

Step 1 – Find the lowest common denominator. Since x is common to both denominators, we can convert the denominator of the second fraction to the LCD by multiplying the numerator and denominator of the second fraction by $(x + 2)$. Step 2 – When both fractions have the LCD, add the numerators to solve.

75) Perform the operation and simplify: $\dfrac{2a^3}{7} \times \dfrac{3}{a^2} = ?$

A) $\dfrac{6a}{7}$ 　　　　B) $\dfrac{5a^3}{7a^2}$ 　　　　C) $\dfrac{2a^6}{21}$ 　　　　D) $\dfrac{21}{2a^6}$

76) $\dfrac{8x + 8}{x^4} \div \dfrac{5x + 5}{x^2} = ?$

A) $\dfrac{5x^2}{8}$ B) $\dfrac{8}{5x^2}$ C) $\dfrac{3x+3}{x^2}$ D) $\dfrac{x^2 + 8x + 8}{x^4 + 5x + 5}$

Factoring Polynomials

77) Factor: $9x^3 - 3x$
   A) $3x(3x^2 - 1)$ B) $3x(3x - 1)$ C) $3x(x^2 - 1)$ D) $3x(x - 3)$

78) Which of the following is a factor of: $2xy - 6x^2y + 4x^2y^2$
   A) $(1 + 3x - 2xy)$ B) $(1 - 3x + 2xy)$ C) $(1 + 3x + 2xy)$ D) $(1 - 3x - 2xy)$

Equivalent Expressions

79) Which of the following mathematical expressions equals $^3/_{xy}$?
   A) $^3/_x \times {}^3/_y$ B) $3 \div 3xy$ C) $3 \div (xy)$ D) $^1/_3 \div 3xy$

80) Which of the following is equivalent to the expression $2(x + 2)(x - 3)$ for all values of x?
   A) $2x^2 - 2x - 12$ B) $2x^2 - 10x - 6$ C) $2x^2 + 2x - 12$ D) $2x^2 + 10x - 6$

81) Which of the following is equivalent to $\dfrac{x}{5} \div \dfrac{9}{y}$?

A) $\dfrac{xy}{45}$ B) $\dfrac{9x}{5y}$ C) $\dfrac{1}{9} \times \dfrac{x}{5y}$ D) $\dfrac{1}{5} \times \dfrac{9}{5y}$

Expanding Polynomials

82) Which of the following expressions is equivalent to $(x + 4y)^2$?

    A) $2(x + 8y)$

    B) $2x + 8y$

    C) $x^2 + 8xy^2 + 16y^2$

    D) $x^2 + 8xy + 16y^2$

83) $\left(2 + \sqrt{6}\right)^2 = ?$

    A) 8

    B) $8 + 2\sqrt{6}$

    C) $8 + 4\sqrt{6}$

    D) $10 + 4\sqrt{6}$

When expanding polynomials, you should use the FOIL method: First – Outside – Inside – Last.
We can demonstrate the FOIL method on an example equation as follows:
$$(a + b)(c + d) =$$
$$(a \times c) + (a \times d) + (b \times c) + (b \times d) =$$
$$ac + ad + bc + bd$$

Linear Equations

84) A student has noticed that the more she studies, the better her grades are. Which of the following graphs illustrates this relationship?

A)

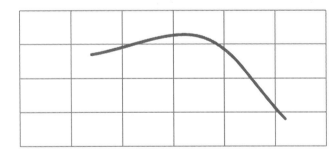

B)

C)

D)

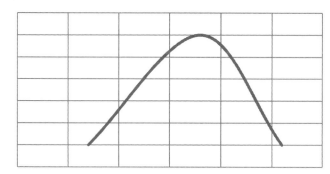

You will need to know the difference between positive linear relationships and negative linear relationships for the exam. In a positive linear relationship, an increase in one variable causes an increase in the other variable, meaning that the line will point upwards from left to right.

In a negative linear relationship, an increase in one variable causes a decrease in the other variable, meaning that the line will point downwards from left to right.

Algebraic Functions

85) The graph of a linear equation is shown below. Which one of the tables of values best represents the points on the graph?

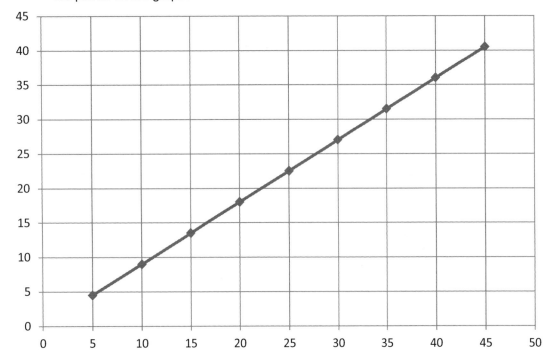

A)

x	y
5	5
10	10
15	15
20	20

B)

x	y
5	4
10	8
15	12
20	16

C)

x	y
5	4.5
10	9
15	13.5
20	18

D)

x	y
5	9
10	13
15	15
20	20

This is an example of an exam question involving algebraic functions. A function expresses the mathematical relationship between x and y. So, a certain recurring mathematical operation on x will yield the output of y. Step 1: Look carefully at the point that is furthest to the left on the graph. You will be able to eliminate several of the answer choices because they will not state this first coordinate correctly. Step 2: Try to work out the relationship between the coordinates of the first point to those of the next point on the line. Use the horizontal and vertical grid lines on the graph to help you.

86) What is the value of $f_1(2)$ where $f_1(x) = 5^x$?

A) 2^5 　　　　 B) 10 　　　　 C) 25 　　　　 D) 25^2

For this type of algebraic function, substitute the value of 2 for x in the second expression.

87) For the two functions $f_1(x)$ and $f_2(x)$, tables of vales are given below. What is the value of $f_2(f_1(2))$?

x	$f_1(x)$
1	3
2	5
3	7
4	9
5	11

x	$f_2(x)$
2	4
3	9
4	16
5	25
6	36

A) 4
B) 5
C) 9
D) 25

Solve the first function for the value of 2. The take the resulting number and put it in as the value of x in the second function.

88) For the functions $f_2(x)$ listed below, x and y are integers greater than 1. If $f_1(x) = x^2$, which of the functions below has the greatest value for $f_1(f_2(x))$?

A) $f_2(x) = x/y$ 　　　　 B) $f_2(x) = y/x$ 　　　　 C) $f_2(x) = xy$ 　　　　 D) $f_2(x) = x - y$

> Look at all of the answer choices, and substitute any positive integers for x and y. Then try the same using negative integers.

89) If $f(x) = x^2 + 3x - 8$, what is $f(x + 3)$?

    A) $(x + 3)^2 + 3x - 8$ C) $x^2 + 3x - 5$

    B) $(x + 3)^2 + 3(x + 3) - 8$ D) $3(x^2 + 3x - 8)$

> In the first equation, substitute $x + 3$ for x to solve.

Logarithmic Functions

90) If $\log_3(x + 2) = 4$, then $x = ?$
    A) 66
    B) 79
    C) 81
    D) 83

> To convert a logarithmic function to an exponent, the number after the equals sign (4 in this problem) becomes the exponent. The small subscript number after "log" (3 in this problem) becomes the base number. Then perform the multiplication to solve. $\log_y Z = x$ is always the same as: $y^x = Z$

Quadratic Equations

91) Simplify: $(x - y)(x + y)$
    A) $x^2 - 2xy - y^2$ B) $x^2 + 2xy - y^2$ C) $x^2 + y^2$ D) $x^2 - y^2$

> Use the FOIL method on quadratic equations like this one when the instructions tell you to simplify. If you do not remember how to perform the FOIL method, look at questions 132 and 133 again. Then try the next question.

92) $(3x + y)(x - 5y) = ?$
    A) $3x^2 - 14xy - 5y^2$ C) $3x^2 + 14xy - 5y^2$

    B) $3x^2 - 14xy + 5y^2$ D) $3x^2 + 14xy + 5y^2$

Linear Inequalities

93) $50 - \dfrac{3x}{5} \geq 41$, then $x \leq ?$

    A) 15   B) 25   C) 41   D) 50

> Step 1: Isolate the whole numbers to one side of the inequality. Step 2: Get rid of the fraction by multiplying each side by 5. Step 3: Divide to simplify further. Step 4: Isolate the variable to solve.

94) The cost of one toy is equal to y. If $x - 2 > 5$ and $y = x - 2$, then the cost of 2 toys is greater than which one of the following?

A) $x - 2$ B) $x - 5$ C) $y + 5$ D) 10

> Look to see if the inequality and the equation have any variables or terms in common. In this problem, both the inequality and the equation contain $x - 2$. The cost of one toy is represented by y, and y is equal to $x - 2$. So, we can substitute values from the equation to the inequality.

Quadratic Inequalities

95) Solve for x: $x^2 - 9 < 0$

A) $x < -3$ or $x > 3$ C) $x < -3$ or $x < 3$
B) $x > -3$ or $x < 3$ D) $x > -3$ or $x > 3$

> For quadratic inequality problems like this one, you need to factor the inequality first. We know that the factors of -9 are: -1×9; -3×3; 1×-9. We do not have a term with only the x variable, so we need factors that add up to zero. $-3 + 3 = 0$. So, try to solve the problem based on these facts. Be sure to check your answer by substituting greater or lesser values (like 4 and -4) into the original inequality.

96) Solve for x: $x^2 - 5x + 6 \leq 0$

A) $2 \geq x \geq 3$ C) $x < -3$ or $x < 2$
B) $2 \leq x \leq 3$ D) $x > -2$ or $x > 3$

> Here is another quadratic inequality problem. Remember to factor the inequality first. We know that the factors of 6 are: 1×6 and 2×3. We have a term with the x variable, so we need factors that add up to five. $2 + 3 = 5$. So, try to solve the problem based on these facts. Be sure to check your work to be sure the signs point the right way by substituting values into the original inequality.

Systems of Equations

97) What ordered pair is a solution to the following system of equations?

$$x + y = 7$$
$$xy = 12$$

A) (2, 6)   B) (6, 2)   C) (4, 2)   D) (3, 4)

> Step 1: Look at the multiplication equation and find the factors of 12. Step 2: Add the factors in each set together to see if they equal 7 to solve the addition in the first equation.

98) Solve by elimination: $3x + 3y = 15$ and $x + 2y = 8$

A) $x = -18$ and $y = 13$ C) $x = 2$ and $y = 3$
B) $x = -2$ and $y = 3$ D) $x = 3$ and $y = 2$

> Step 1: Look at the x term of the first equation, which is $3x$. In order to eliminate the x variable, we need to multiply the second equation by 3. Step 2: Subtract this result from the first equation to solve.

Sequences and Series

99)   What is the next number in the following sequence?   1, 5, 9, 13, 17, . . .

      A) 20   B) 21   C) 30   D) 40

Sequences are numbers in a list like the following: 1, 3, 5, 7, 9. In a series, the numbers are added: 1 + 3 + 5 + 7 + 9. In an arithmetic sequence, the difference between one number and the next is known as a constant. In other words, you add the same value each time until you reach the end of the sequence. The formula for the nth number of an arithmetic sequence is $a + [d \times (n - 1)]$, where variable a represents the starting number and variable d represents the difference or constant.

---

100)   What is the next number in the following sequence?   2, 6, 18, 54, . . .

      A) 60   B) 72   C) 80   D) 162

When the sequence cannot be solved by addition, then you usually have a geometric sequence.

In a geometric sequence, each number is found by multiplying the previous term by a factor known as a common ratio. Where the first number is represented by variable a and the factor (called the "common ratio") is represented by variable r, the formula for calculating the nth item in a geometric sequence is: $ar^{(n-1)}$

Bonus Exercises – Solutions and Explanations

1) The correct answer is C. The problem is asking for the total for all three years, so we add the three figures together: $25,135 + $32,787 + $47,004 = $104,926

2) The correct answer is D. For questions that ask you to calculate the change given to a customer, you need to take the amount of money the customer gives the cashier and subtract the amount of the purchase: $50.00 – $41.28 = $8.72

3) The correct answer is D. Multiplication problems will often include the words 'each' or 'every.' The problem states that the salesperson earns a $175 referral fee on every customer, so the referral fee was earned 8 times this month. We need to multiply the amount of the referral fee by the number of customers to solve: $175 × 8 = $1400

4) The correct answer is C. Division problems will often include the word 'per.' The problem states that the employee works 30 hours per week. So, we divide the total weekly amount by the number of hours to solve: $535.50 ÷ 30 = $17.85

5) The correct answer is B. When you have to add a negative number to a positive number, you are really subtracting. So, add the business profits and subtract the business losses:
953 + 1502 – 286 – 107 = 2062

6) The correct answer is A. In this problem, we need to subtract the excess of the depth of Lake Bajo from the location below sea level of Lake Alto. The location below sea level of Lake Alto is a negative number, so we subtract as follows: –35 – 62 = –97. Remember to express your result as a negative number.

7) The correct answer is B. In order to express a fraction as a decimal, treat the line in the fraction as the division symbol: 3/5 = 3 ÷ 5 = 0.60. Be careful with the decimal placement in your final result.

8) The correct answer is C. To express a decimal number as a percent, move the decimal point two places to the right and add the percent sign: 0.55 = 55.0%

9) The correct answer is D. In order to express a fraction as a percentage, you need to divide and then express the result as a percentage. Step 1 – Treat the line in the fraction as the division symbol: 5/14 = 5 ÷ 14 = 0.357. Step 2 – To express the result from Step 1 as a percentage, we need to move the decimal point two places to the right and add the percent sign: 0.357 = 35.7%

10) The correct answer is D. For your exam, you should be able to recognize the equivalent fractions for commonly-used decimal numbers. If you are unsure, perform division on the answer choices to check:
3/4 = 3 ÷ 4 = 0.75

11) The correct answer is A. For your exam, you should be able to recognize the equivalent fractions for commonly-used percentages. If you are unsure, perform division on the answer choices to check:
1/3 = 1 ÷ 3 = 0.3333 = 33%

12) The correct answer is C. Any given percentage is out of 100%, so we divide by 100 to express a percentage as a decimal. So, move the decimal point two places to the left and remove the percent sign:
45% = 45 ÷ 100 = 0.45

13) The correct answer is B. Express both amounts as decimal numbers and multiply to solve:
14^{1}/$_{4}$ pounds × 36 cents per pound = 14.25 × 0.36 = $5.13

14) The correct answer is C. There are 60 minutes in an hour, so multiply the minutes in the hour by the decimal number given in the problem to solve: 60 minutes × 0.35 hour = 60 × 0.35 = 21 minutes

15) The correct answer is A. Step 1 – Subtract the discount from the original price: $24 – $5 = $19. Step 2 – Take the result from Step 1 and multiply by the number of units sold: $19 × 12 = $228

16) The correct answer is D. Step 1 – Determine the total number of hours worked: 7 hours per day for 4 days = 7 × 4 = 28 hours. Step 2 – Calculate the profit the company makes per hour. The customer was billed $45 per hour for the employee's work, and he was paid $25 per hour: $45 – $25 = $20 profit per hour. Step 3 – Multiply the total number of hours by the profit per hour to solve: 28 hours × $20 profit per hour 28 × 20 = $560

17) The correct answer is A. Step 1 – Calculate how many minutes there are in 40 hours: 40 hours × 60 minutes per hour = 2400 minutes. Step 2 – Divide the amount of prescriptions into the previous result to get the rate: 2400 ÷ 250 = 9.6 minutes per prescription

18) The correct answer is C. Take the amount of orders that were delivered on time and divide by the amount of total orders: 105 ÷ 120 = 0.875 = 87.5%

19) The correct answer is B. On Monday cell growth was 27, and for all of the days Tuesday through Friday, cell attrition was 13 per day. Step 1 – Cell attrition is a negative number, so perform multiplication to get the total for the four days (Tuesday through Friday): –13 × 4 = –52. Step 2 – On Monday cell growth was 27, so add this to the result from Step 1 to solve: –52 + 27 = –25

20) The correct answer is B. To find the average, you need to find the total, and then divide the total by the number of hours. Step 1 – Find the total: 23 + 25 + 26 + 24 + 22 = 120. Step 2 – Divide the result from Step 1 by the number of hours: 120 ÷ 5 = 24

21) The correct answer is D. Step 1 – Take the 66 units of cement powder for the current batch and divide by the 3 units stated in the original ratio: 22 ÷ 3 = 22. Step 2 – Multiply the result from Step 1 by the 2 units of sand stated in the original ratio to get your answer: 2 × 22 = 44

22) The correct answer is D. The problem states that we are working with a ratio, so the employees and the supervisors form separate groups. Step 1 – Add the two groups together: 50 + 1 = 51. Step 2 – Take the total amount of employees stated in the problem and divide this by the figure calculated in Step 1 to get the amount of supervisors: 255 ÷ 51 = 5

23) The correct answer is D. The problem uses the phrase '2 out of every 20 employees' so we know that there are 2 employees who form a subset within each group of 20. Step 1 – Take the total number of employees and divide this by 20: 480 ÷ 20 = 24. Step 2 – Take the result from Step 1 and multiply by the amount in the subset to solve: 24 × 2 = 48

24) The correct answer is C. Step 1 – Calculate the amount of time spent on the initial job to do 3 wheel covers: 8:10 to 8:22 = 12 minutes. Step 2 – Calculate how many minutes are needed to change 1 wheel cover: 12 minutes ÷ 3 = 4 minutes each. Step 3 – Divide the figure from Step 2 into 60 minutes to solve: 60 ÷ 4 = 15

25) The correct answer is C. Step 1 – Add the whole numbers. The whole numbers are the numbers in front of the fractions: 15 + 13 = 28. Step 2 – Add the fractions. If you have two fractions that have the same denominator, you add the numerators and keep the common denominator: 2/8 + 5/8 = 7/8. Step 3 – Combine the results from Step 1 and Step 2 to get your new mixed number to solve the problem: 28 + 7/8 = 28$^7/_8$

26) The correct answer is A. Step 1 – Add the whole numbers: 2 + 4 = 6. Step 2 – Add the fractions. If you have two fractions that have the same denominator, you add the numerators and keep the common denominator: 1/8 + 3/8 = 4/8. Step 3 – Simplify the fraction from Step 2: 4/8 = (4 ÷ 4)/(8 ÷ 4) = 1/2. Step 4 – Combine the results from Step 1 and Step 3 to get your new mixed number to solve the problem: 6 + 1/2 = $6^1/_2$

27) The correct answer is A. Step 1 – Subtract the whole numbers: 5 – 4 = 1. Step 2 – Subtract the fractions. If you have two fractions that have the same denominator, you subtract the numerators and keep the common denominator: 3/16 – 1/16 = 2/16. Step 3 – Simplify the fraction from Step 2: 2/16 = (2 ÷ 2)/(16 ÷ 2) = 1/8. Step 4 – Combine the results from Step 1 and Step 3 to get your new mixed number to solve the problem: 1 + 1/8 = $1^1/_8$

28) The correct answer is B. Add the three figures together to solve: 0.25 + 0.50 + 0.10 = 0.85. Remember to be sure to put the decimal point in the correct place when you work out the solution to problems like this one.

29) The correct answer is C. Add the percentages together to solve: 25% + 50% = 75%

30) The correct answer is D. Step 1 – Multiply the whole numbers: 5 × 1 = 5. Step 2 – Multiply the whole number by the fraction: 5 × 1/4 = 5/4. Step 3 – Convert the fraction from Step 2 to a mixed number: 5/4 = $1^1/_4$. Step 4 – Combine the results from Step 1 and Step 3 to get your new mixed number: 5 + $1^1/_4$ = $6^1/_4$. Step 5 – Convert the result from Step 4 to hours and minutes: $6^1/_4$ hours = 6 hours and 15 minutes

31) The correct answer is B. Step 1 – Convert the first fraction to the common denominator: 1/8 = (1 × 4)/(8 × 4) = 4/32. Step 2 – Add one more increment to this to get your result: 4/32 + 1/32 = 5/32

32) The correct answer is A. Step 1 – Work out the cost for the first supplier: 50 units × $0.50 = $25. Step 2 – Compare to other deals to solve: The other deals are $27.50 and $30, so $25 is the best deal.

33) The correct answer is D. Step 1 – Determine the duration of the stay in weeks and nights: 9 nights = 1 week + 2 nights. Step 2 – Add the cost for 1 week to the cost for 2 days to solve: $280 + (2 × $45) = $280 + $90 = $370

34) The correct answer is D. Step 1 – Determine the dollar value of the discount: $15 – $12 = $3. Step 2 – Divide the result from Step 1 by the original price to get the percentage: $3 ÷ $15 = 0.20 = 20%

35) The correct answer is C. Step 1 – Determine the dollar value of the markup on the mug: $9 retail price – $3 cost = $6 markup. Step 2 – Calculate the percentage of the markup by dividing the dollar value of the markup by the cost: $6 ÷ $3 = 2.00 = 200%. Step 3 – Use the percentage markup from the previous step to determine the dollar value of the markup on the bowl: $4 × 200% = $4 × 2 = $8. Step 4 – Add the dollar value of the markup for the bowl to the cost of the bowl to get the retail price: $8 + $4 = $12

36) The correct answer is D. To calculate a reverse percentage you need to divide, rather than multiply. So, take the $20 discount and divide by the 25% percentage: $20 ÷ 25% = $20 ÷ 0.25 = $80

37) The correct answer is C. Step 1 – Add the times for the first two processes and express in terms of hours and minutes: Production time of 3 hours and 25 minutes + Bottling and labeling time of 1 hour and 40 minutes = 3 hours + 1 hour + 25 minutes + 40 minutes = 4 hours and 65 minutes = 5 hours and 5 minutes. Step 2 – Add the time for the packaging process of 26 hours to the result from Step 1: 5 hours and 5 minutes + 26 hours = 31 hours and 5 minutes. Step 3 – Determine the time that the batch will be ready for shipment. 31 hours and 5 minutes have passed. In other words, a period of 24 hours and an additional 7 hours and 5 minutes have passed. The process started on Monday at 10:30 am, so by

169

Tuesday at 10:30 am, 24 hours will have passed. An additional 7 hours and 5 minutes takes us to Tuesday at 5:35 pm.

38) The correct answer is C. Step 1 – Determine the cost from the first supplier: 240 × 0.25 = $60. The tax on this will be $60 × 6.5% = $60 × 0.065 = $3.90. Then add the tax to the cost to get the total: $60 + $3.90 = $63.90. Step 2 – Determine the total cost from the second supplier: $58 cost + ($58 × 0.065 tax) = $58 + 3.77 = $61.77. So, you will get the better deal from the second supplier at $61.77.

39) The correct answer is D. Step 1 – Determine how many days are needed to make the small frames. 20 small frames can be made in 4 days: 20 frames ÷ 4 days = 5 small frames per day. The customer wants 40 small frames, so divide by the rate to determine how many days are going to be needed for the small frames: 40 frames ÷ 5 per day = 8 days. Step 2 – Determine how many days are going to be needed to make the large frames. 21 larges frames can be made in 3 days: 21 ÷ 3 = 7 large frames per day. 64 large frames need to be made for the order: 64 ÷ 7 = 9.1 days. Step 3 – Add the results from the two previous steps to solve: 8 days + 9.1 days = 17.1 days, which we round down to 17 days.

40) The correct answer is C. Step 1 – Calculate the percentage of work completed per day. 12.5% of the work has been completed in 4 days: 12.5 % ÷ 4 days = 3.125% per day. Step 2 – Determine how many days in total are needed to complete the entire job by dividing 100% by the result from the previous step: 100% ÷ 3.125% = 32 days. Step 3 – Determine the number of days remaining: 32 days in total – 4 days completed = 28 days remaining

41) The correct answer is D. Step 1 – Add the feet together: 123 + 138 = 261 feet. Step 2 – Add the inches together: 6 + 8 = 14 inches. Step 3 – Convert the inches to feet and inches if the result from Step 2 is 12 inches or more: 14 inches = 1 foot 2 inches. Step 4 – Combine the results from Step 1 and Step 3 to solve: 261 feet + 1 foot 2 inches = 262 feet 2 inches

42) The correct answer is A. Step 1 – Convert the weight of the full box from pounds and ounces to just ounces. We are using the formula 1 pound = 16 ounces, so 8 pounds and 5 ounces = (8 × 16) + 5 = 128 + 5 = 133 ounces. Step 2 – The problem states that the box weighs 7 ounces when it is empty. So, subtract the weight of the empty box from the weight of the full box to get the weight of the product inside the box: 133 ounces – 7 ounces = 126 ounces. Step 3 – The problem tells us that each supplement weighs 0.75 ounces. Take the total weight from the previous step and divide by the weight per unit to determine how many units the box contains: 126 ounces ÷ 0.75 ounces = 168 units

43) The correct answer is B. Step 1 – Calculate the amount of remaining stock in inches: (2 × 75 inches) + (4 × 25.25 inches) = 150 + 101 = 251 inches. Step 2 – Convert the existing stock from inches to yards: 1 foot = 12 inches and 1 yard = 3 feet, so there are 36 inches in 1 yard. So, divide the amount of inches by 36 to convert to yards: 251 ÷ 36 = 6.97 yards. Step 3 – Calculate the amount required to restock. 60 yards are required in total, and there are 6.97 yards on hand, so subtract to find out how many more yards are needed to get the stock back up to 60 yards: 60 – 6.97 = 53.03 yards needed. Step 4 – The yarn comes in 5-yard balls, so calculate how many balls to buy to cover the 53.03 yards that are required: 53.03 ÷ 5 = 10.6 balls. It is not possible to buy a fractional part of a ball, so we round up to 11 balls.

44) The correct answer is A. Our points are (5, 2) and (7, 4), so substitute the values into the midpoint formula.
$(x_1 + x_2) ÷ 2 , (y_1 + y_2) ÷ 2$
$(5 + 7) ÷ 2$ = midpoint x, $(2 + 4) ÷ 2$ = midpoint y
$12 ÷ 2$ = midpoint x, $6 ÷ 2$ = midpoint y
6 = midpoint x, 3 = midpoint y

45) The correct answer is B. First, find the midpoint of the x coordinates for (**−4**, 2) and (**8**,−6).

midpoint $x = (x_1 + x_2) \div 2$

midpoint $x = (−4 + 8) \div 2$

midpoint $x = 4 \div 2$

midpoint $x = 2$

Then find the midpoint of the y coordinates for (−4, **2**) and (8,**−6**).

midpoint $y = (y_1 + y_2) \div 2$

midpoint $y = (2 + −6) \div 2$

midpoint $y = −4 \div 2$

midpoint $y = −2$

So, the midpoint is (2, −2)

46) The correct answer is D. Substitute the values (2, 3) and (6, 7) into the formula.

$d = \sqrt{(x_2 − x_1)^2 + (y_2 − y_1)^2}$

$d = \sqrt{(6 − 2)^2 + (7 − 3)^2}$

$d = \sqrt{4^2 + 4^2}$

$d = \sqrt{16 + 16}$

$d = \sqrt{32}$

47) The correct answer is A. Substitute the values into the slope-intercept formula.

$y = mx + b$

$315 = m5 + 15$

$315 − 15 = m5 + 15 − 15$

$300 = m5$

$300 \div 5 = m5 \div 5$

$60 = m$

48) The correct answer is A. As y increases by 5, x decreases by 5. So, the slope is −1. The line includes point (20, 15), which is the fifth point from the left.

49) The correct answer is A. Remember that the y intercept is where the line crosses the y axis, so $x = 0$ for the y intercept. Begin by substituting 0 for x.

$y = x + 14$

$y = 0 + 14$

$y = 14$

Therefore, the coordinates (0, 14) represent the y intercept.

On the other hand, the x intercept exists where the line crosses the x axis, so $y = 0$ for the x intercept.

Now substitute 0 for y.

$y = x + 14$

$0 = x + 14$

$0 - 14 = x + 14 - 14$

$-14 = x$

So, the coordinates (−14, 0) represent the x intercept.

50) The correct answer is A. The x intercept is the point at which a line crosses the x axis of a graph. In order for the line to cross the x axis, y must be equal to zero at that particular point of the graph. On the other hand, the y intercept is the point at which the line crosses the y axis. So, in order for the line to cross the y axis, x must be equal to zero at that particular point of the graph. First, substitute 0 for y in order to find the x intercept.

$x^2 + 2y^2 = 144$

$x^2 + (2 \times 0) = 144$

$x^2 + 0 = 144$

$x^2 = 144$

$x = 12$

Then substitute 0 for x in order to find the y intercept.

$x^2 + 2y^2 = 144$

$(0 \times 0) + 2y^2 = 144$

$0 + 2y^2 = 144$

$2y^2 \div 2 = 144 \div 2$

$y^2 = 72$

$y = \sqrt{72}$

So, the y intercept is $(0, \sqrt{72})$ and the x intercept is (12, 0).

51) The correct answer is C. Substitute −2 for x to solve.
$2x^2 - x + 5 =$
$[2 \times (-2^2)] - (-2) + 5 =$
$[2 \times (4)] - (-2) + 5 =$
$(2 \times 4) + 2 + 5 =$
$8 + 2 + 5 = 15$

52) The correct answer is B. Isolate x to solve. You do this by doing the same operation on each side of the equation.
$-6x + 5 = -19$
Subtract 5 from each side to get rid of the integer 5 on the left side.

$-6x + 5 - 5 = -19 - 5$
Then simplify.
$-6x = -24$
Then divide each side by –6 to isolate x.
$-6x \div -6 = -24 \div -6$
$x = -24 \div -6$
$x = 4$

53) The correct answer is B.
Remember to do multiplication on the items in parentheses first.
$4x - 3(x + 2) = -3$
$4x - 3x - 6 = -3$
Then deal with the integers.
$4x - 3x - 6 + 6 = -3 + 6$
$4x - 3x = 3$
Then solve for x.
$4x - 3x = 3$
$x = 3$

54) The correct answer is C. Isolate the integers to one side of the equation.

$\frac{3}{4}x - 2 = 4$

$\frac{3}{4}x - 2 + 2 = 4 + 2$

$\frac{3}{4}x = 6$

Then get rid of the fraction by multiplying both sides by the denominator.

$\frac{3}{4}x \times 4 = 6 \times 4$

$3x = 24$

Then divide to solve the problem.

$3x \div 3 = 24 \div 3$

$x = 8$

55) The correct answer is B. Substitute 1 for x: $\frac{x-3}{2-x} = \frac{1-3}{2-1} = (1 - 3) \div (2 - 1) = -2 \div 1 = -2$

56) The correct answer is B.
Substitute 5 for the value of x to solve.
$x^2 + xy - y = 41$
$5^2 + 5y - y = 41$
$25 + 5y - y = 41$
$25 - 25 + 5y - y = 41 - 25$
$5y - y = 16$

173

$4y = 16$
$4y \div 4 = 16 \div 4$
$y = 4$

57) The correct answer is B. Substitute 12 for the value of x. Then simplify and solve.
$x^2 + xy - y = 254$
$12^2 + 12y - y = 254$
$144 + 12y - y = 254$
$144 - 144 + 12y - y = 254 - 144$
$12y - y = 110$
$11y = 110$
$11y \div 11 = 110 \div 11$
$y = 10$

58) The correct answer is C.
$6 + 8(2\sqrt{x} + 4) = 62$
$6 - 6 + 8(2\sqrt{x} + 4) = 62 - 6$
$8(2\sqrt{x} + 4) = 56$
$16\sqrt{x} + 32 = 56$
$16\sqrt{x} + 32 - 32 = 56 - 32$
$16\sqrt{x} = 24$
$16\sqrt{x} \div 16 = 24 \div 16$
$\sqrt{x} = 24 \div 16$
$\sqrt{x} = \dfrac{24}{16}$
$\sqrt{x} = \dfrac{24 \div 8}{16 \div 8} = \dfrac{3}{2}$

59) The correct answer is D. The factors of 50 are: $1 \times 50 = 50$; $2 \times 25 = 50$; $5 \times 10 = 50$. If any of your factors are perfect squares, you can simplify the radical. 25 is a perfect square, so, you need to factor inside the radical sign as shown to solve the problem: $\sqrt{50} = \sqrt{25 \times 2} = \sqrt{5^2 \times 2} = \sqrt{5^2} \times \sqrt{2} = 5\sqrt{2}$

60) The correct answer is D. 36 is the common factor, So, factor the amounts inside the radicals and simplify:

$\sqrt{36} + 4\sqrt{72} - 2\sqrt{144} =$

$\sqrt{36} + 4\sqrt{36 \times 2} - 2\sqrt{36 \times 4} =$

$\sqrt{6 \times 6} + 4\sqrt{(6 \times 6) \times 2} - 2\sqrt{(6 \times 6) \times 4} =$
$6 + (4 \times 6)\sqrt{2} - (2 \times 6)\sqrt{4} =$
$6 + 24\sqrt{2} - (12 \times 2) =$

174

$$6 + 24\sqrt{2} - 24 =$$
$$-18 + 24\sqrt{2}$$

61) The correct answer is A. $\sqrt{7} \times \sqrt{11} = \sqrt{7 \times 11} = \sqrt{77}$

62) The correct answer is B. Add the numbers in front of the radical signs to solve. If there is no number before the radical, then put in the number 1 because then the radical will count only 1 time when you add.
$$\sqrt{15} + 3\sqrt{15} = 1\sqrt{15} + 3\sqrt{15} = (1+3)\sqrt{15} = 4\sqrt{15}$$

63) The correct answer is B. The cube root is the number which satisfies the equation when multiplied by itself two times: $\sqrt[3]{\dfrac{216}{27}} = \sqrt[3]{\dfrac{6 \times 6 \times 6}{3 \times 3 \times 3}} = \dfrac{6}{3} = 2$

64) The correct answer is A. The base number is 7. Add the exponents: $7^5 \times 7^3 = 7^{(5+3)} = 7^8$

65) The correct answer is B. The base is xy. Subtract the exponents: $xy^6 \div xy^3 = xy^{(6-3)} = xy^3$

66) The correct answer is C. Perform the operation on the radicals and then simplify.
$$\sqrt{8x^4} \cdot \sqrt{32x^6} = \sqrt{8x^4 \times 32x^6} = \sqrt{256x^{10}} = \sqrt{16 \times 16 \times x^5 \times x^5} = 16x^5$$

67) The correct answer is B. We have the base number of 10 and we are multiplying, so we can add the exponent of 5 to the exponent of −1: (1.7 × 10^5 miles per hour) × (2 × 10^{-1} hours) = 1.7 × 2 × 10$^{(5+-1)}$ = 3.4 × 10^4 = 3.4 × 10,000 = 34,000 miles

68) The correct answer is D. When you have a fraction as an exponent, the numerator is new exponent and the denominator goes in front as the root: $\sqrt{x^{\frac{5}{7}}} = \left(\sqrt[7]{x}\right)^5$

69) The correct answer is B. The principle is that $x^{-b} = \dfrac{1}{x^b}$. Accordingly, $x^{-5} = \dfrac{1}{x^5}$

70) The correct answer is B. Following the principle mentioned in the answer to question 119, $(-4)^{-3} = \dfrac{1}{-4^3} = -\dfrac{1}{64}$

71) The correct answer is C. Any non-zero number raised to the power of zero is equal to 1.

72) The correct answer is C. Any non-zero number multiplied by a variable and raised to the power of zero is equal to 1.

73) The correct answer is C.

$$\frac{b + \frac{2}{7}}{\frac{1}{b}} = \left(b + \frac{2}{7}\right) \div \frac{1}{b} = \left(b + \frac{2}{7}\right) \times \frac{b}{1} = b\left(b + \frac{2}{7}\right) = b^2 + \frac{2b}{7}$$

74) The correct answer is D. Find the lowest common denominator for the second fraction. Then add the numerators.

$$\frac{x^2}{x^2+2x}+\frac{8}{x}=\frac{x^2}{x^2+2x}+\left(\frac{8}{x}\times\frac{x+2}{x+2}\right)=\frac{x^2}{x^2+2x}+\frac{8x+16}{x^2+2x}=\frac{x^2+8x+16}{x^2+2x}$$

75) The correct answer is A. Multiply as shown: $\dfrac{2a^3}{7}\times\dfrac{3}{a^2}=\dfrac{2a^3\times3}{7\times a^2}=\dfrac{6a^3}{7a^2}$

Then find the greatest common factor and cancel out to simplify: $\dfrac{6a^3}{7a^2}=\dfrac{6a\times a^2}{7\times a^2}=\dfrac{6a\times a^2}{7\times a^2}=\dfrac{6a}{7}$

76) The correct answer is B. Invert and multiply.

$$\frac{8x+8}{x^4}\div\frac{5x+5}{x^2}=\frac{8x+8}{x^4}\times\frac{x^2}{5x+5}=\frac{(8x\times x^2)+(8\times x^2)}{(x^4\times5x)+(x^4\times5)}=\frac{8x^3+8x^2}{5x^5+5x^4}$$

Then factor out $(x + 1)$ from the numerator and denominator and cancel out:

$$\frac{8x^3+8x^2}{5x^5+5x^4}=\frac{(8x^2\times x)+(8x^2\times1)}{(5x^4\times x)+(5x^4\times1)}=\frac{8x^2(x+1)}{5x^4(x+1)}=\frac{8x^2(x+1)}{5x^4(x+1)}=\frac{8x^2}{5x^4}$$

Finally, factor out x^2 and cancel it out: $\dfrac{8x^2}{5x^4}=\dfrac{x^2\times8}{x^2\times5x^2}=\dfrac{x^2\times8}{x^2\times5x^2}=\dfrac{8}{5x^2}$

77) The correct answer is A. The factors of 9 are: $1\times9=9$; $3\times3=9$. The factors of 3 are: $1\times3=3$. So, put the integer for the common factor outside the parentheses first: $9x^3-3x=3(3x^3-x)$
Then determine if there are any common variables for the terms that remain in the parentheses.
For $(3x^2-x)$ the terms $3x^2$ and x have the variable x in common. So, now factor out x to solve:
$3(3x^3-x)=3x(3x^2-1)$

78) The correct answer is B. Looking at this expression, we can see that each term contains x. We can also see that each term contains y. So, first factor out xy: $2xy-6x^2y+4x^2y^2=xy(2-6x+4xy)$. We can also see that all of the terms inside the parentheses are divisible by 2. Now let's factor out the 2. To do this, we divide each term inside the parentheses by 2: $xy(2-6x+4xy)=2xy(1-3x+2xy)$

79) The correct answer is C. The line in a fraction is the same as the division symbol. For example, $^a/_b=a\div b$. In the same way, $^3/_{xy}=3\div(xy)$.

80) The correct answer is A. You should use the FOIL method in this problem. Be very careful with the negative numbers when doing the multiplication.
$2(x+2)(x-3)=$
$2[(x\times x)+(x\times-3)+(2\times x)+(2\times-3)]=$
$2(x^2+-3x+2x+-6)=$
$2(x^2-3x+2x-6)=$
$2(x^2-x-6)$

Then multiply each term by the 2 at the front of the parentheses.
$2(x^2-x-6)=$
$2x^2-2x-12$

81) The correct answer is A. To divide, invert the second fraction and then multiply as shown.

$$\frac{x}{5} \div \frac{9}{y} = \frac{x}{5} \times \frac{y}{9} = \frac{x \times y}{5 \times 9} = \frac{xy}{45}$$

82) The correct answer is D. Use the FOIL method to expand the polynomial.

FIRST – Multiply the first term from the first set of parentheses by the first term from the second set of parentheses: $(\mathbf{x} + 4y)(\mathbf{x} + 4y) = x \times x = x^2$

OUTSIDE – Multiply the first term from the first set of parentheses by the second term from the second set of parentheses: $(\mathbf{x} + 4y)(x + \mathbf{4y}) = x \times 4y = 4xy$

INSIDE – Multiply the second term from the first set of parentheses by the first term from the second set of parentheses: $(x + \mathbf{4y})(\mathbf{x} + 4y) = 4y \times x = 4xy$

LAST– Multiply the second term from the first set of parentheses by the second term from the second set of parentheses: $(x + \mathbf{4y})(x + \mathbf{4y}) = 4y \times 4y = 16y^2$

Finally, we add all of the products together: $x^2 + 4xy + 4xy + 16y^2 = x^2 + 8xy + 16y^2$

83) The correct answer is D. $\left(2 + \sqrt{6}\right)^2 = \left(2 + \sqrt{6}\right)\left(2 + \sqrt{6}\right) =$
$\left(2 \times 2\right) + \left(2 \times \sqrt{6}\right) + \left(2 \times \sqrt{6}\right) + \left(\sqrt{6} \times \sqrt{6}\right) = 4 + 4\sqrt{6} + 6 = 10 + 4\sqrt{6}$

84) The correct answer is C. As the studying increases, the grades also increase. A positive linear relationship therefore exists between the two variables. This is represented in chart C.

85) The correct answer is C. We can see that the line does not begin on exactly on (5, 5), nor does it begin on (5, 9) because the first point is slightly below the horizontal line for $y = 5$. Therefore, we can rule out answers A and D. If we look at $x = 20$ on the graph, we can see that $y = 18$ at this point. We can express this as the function: $f(x) = x \times 0.9$. Putting in the values of x from chart (C), we get the following: $5 \times 0.9 = 4.5$; $10 \times 0.9 = 9$; $15 \times 0.9 = 13.5$; $20 \times 0.9 = 18$. This is represented in table C.

86) The correct answer is C. Put the value provided for x into the function to solve.
$$f_1(2) = 5^x = 5^2 = 25$$

87) The correct answer is D. First, solve for the function in the inner-most set of parentheses, in this case $f_1(x)$. To solve, you simply have to look at the first table. Find the value of 2 in the first column and the related value in the second column. For $x = 2$, $f_1(2) = 5$. Then, take this new value to solve for $f_2(x)$. Look at the second table. Find the value of 5 in the first column and the related value in the second column. For $x = 5$, $f_2(5) = 25$.

88) The correct answer is C. Two whole numbers that are greater than 1 will always result in a greater number when they are multiplied by each other, rather than when those numbers are divided by each other or subtracted from each other. So, for positive integers, $x \times y$ will always be greater than the following:

$x \div y$

$y \div x$

$x - y$

$y - x$

$1 \div x$

$1 \div y$

89) The correct answer is B. Substitute $x + 3$ for x in the original function to solve. So, $x^2 + 3x - 8$ becomes $(x + 3)^2 + 3(x + 3) - 8$

90) The correct answer is B. First, you need to convert the logarithmic function into an exponential equation. To convert a logarithmic function to an exponent, the number after the equals sign (4 in this problem) becomes the exponent. The small subscript number after "log" (3 in this problem) becomes the base number. So, the exponential equation for $\log_3(x + 2) = 4$ is $3^4 = x + 2$. Then find the result for the exponent: $3^4 = 3 \times 3 \times 3 \times 3 = 81$. Substituting 81 on the left side of the equation, we get $81 = x + 2$. Therefore, $x = 79$.

91) The correct answer is D. If a term or variable is subtracted within the parentheses, you have to keep the negative sign with it when you multiply.
FIRST: $(\boldsymbol{x} - y)(\boldsymbol{x} + y) = x \times x = x^2$
OUTSIDE: $(\boldsymbol{x} - y)(x + \boldsymbol{y}) = x \times y = xy$
INSIDE: $(x - \boldsymbol{y})(\boldsymbol{x} + y) = -y \times x = -xy$
LAST: $(x - \boldsymbol{y})(x + \boldsymbol{y}) = -y \times y = -y^2$
SOLUTION: $x^2 + xy + - xy - y^2 = x^2 - y^2$

92) The correct answer is A.
FIRST: $(\boldsymbol{3x} + y)(\boldsymbol{x} - 5y) = 3x \times x = 3x^2$
OUTSIDE: $(\boldsymbol{3x} + y)(x - \boldsymbol{5y}) = 3x \times -5y = -15xy$
INSIDE: $(3x + \boldsymbol{y})(\boldsymbol{x} - 5y) = y \times x = xy$
LAST: $(3x + \boldsymbol{y})(x - \boldsymbol{5y}) = y \times -5y = -5y^2$
Then add all of the above once you have completed FOIL: $3x^2 - 15xy + xy - 5y^2 = 3x^2 - 14xy - 5y^2$

93) The correct answer is A. First, Isolate the whole numbers.
$50 - \frac{3x}{5} \geq 41$
$(50 - 50) - \frac{3x}{5} \geq 41 - 50$
$-\frac{3x}{5} \geq -9$

Then get rid of the denominator on the fraction.
$-\frac{3x}{5} \geq -9$
$\left(5 \times -\frac{3x}{5}\right) \geq -9 \times 5$
$-3x \geq -9 \times 5$
$-3x \geq -45$
Then isolate the remaining whole numbers.
$-3x \geq -45$
$-3x \div 3 \geq -45 \div 3$
$-x \geq -45 \div 3$
$-x \geq -15$
Then deal with the negative number.
$-x \geq -15$
$-x + 15 \geq -15 + 15$
$-x + 15 \geq 0$

Finally, isolate the unknown variable as a positive number.
$-x + 15 \geq 0$
$-x + x + 15 \geq 0 + x$
$15 \geq x$
$x \leq 15$

94) The correct answer is D. Substitute 5 for $x - 2$ as shown: $x - 2 > 5$ and $x - 2 = y$, so $y > 5$. If two toys are being purchased, we need to solve for $2y$:

$y \times 2 > 5 \times 2$

$2y > 10$

95) The correct answer is B. For quadratic inequality problems like this one, you need to factor the inequality first. The factors of -9 are: -1×9; -3×3; 1×-9. Because we do not have a term with only the x variable, we need factors that add up to zero, so factor as shown:
$x^2 - 9 < 0$
$(x + 3)(x - 3) < 0$

Then find values for x by solving each parenthetical for 0.
$(x + 3) = 0$
$(-3 + 3) = 0$
$x = -3$

$(x - 3) = 0$
$(3 - 3) = 0$
$x = 3$
So, $x > -3$ or $x < 3$

You can then check your work to be sure that you have the inequality signs pointing the right way.
Use -2 to check $x > -3$. Since $-2 > -3$ is correct, our proof should also be correct:
$x^2 - 9 < 0$
$-2^2 - 9 < 0$
$4 - 9 < 0$
$-5 < 0$ CORRECT

Use 4 to check for $x < 3$. Since $4 < 3$ is incorrect, our proof should also be incorrect.
$x^2 - 9 < 0$
$4^2 - 9 < 0$
$16 - 9 < 0$
$7 < 0$ INCORRECT

Therefore, we have checked that $x > -3$ or $x < 3$.

96) The correct answer is B.
Factor: $x^2 - 5x + 6 \leq 0$
$(x - 2)(x - 3) \leq 0$

Then solve each parenthetical for zero:
$(x - 2) = 0$
$2 - 2 = 0$

x = 2
(x − 3) = 0
3 − 3 = 0
x = 3
So, $2 \leq x \leq 3$

Now check. Use 1 to check to $2 \leq x$, which is the same as $x \geq 2$. Since 1 is not actually greater than or equal to 2, our proof for this should be incorrect.

$x^2 - 5x + 6 \leq 0$
$1^2 - (5 \times 1) + 6 \leq 0$
$1 - 5 + 6 \leq 0$
$-4 + 6 \leq 0$
$2 \leq 0$ INCORRECT

Use 2.5 to check for $x \leq 3$. Since 2.5 really is less than 3, our proof should be correct.
$x^2 - 5x + 6 \leq 0$
$2.5^2 - (5 \times 2.5) + 6 \leq 0$
$6.25 - 12.5 + 6 \leq 0$
$-0.25 \leq 0$ CORRECT

Therefore, we have checked that $2 \leq x \leq 3$

97) The correct answer is D. We know that the products of 12 are: $1 \times 12 = 12$; $2 \times 6 = 12$; $3 \times 4 = 12$. So, add each of the two factors together to solve the first equation: $1 + 12 = 13$; $2 + 6 = 8$; $3 + 4 = 7$. (3, 4) solves both equations, so it is the correct answer.

98) The correct answer is C. The first term of the second equation is x. To eliminate the x variable, we need to multiply the second equation by 3 because the first equation contains 3x.
$x + 2y = 8$
$(3 \times x) + (3 \times 2y) = (3 \times 8)$
$3x + 6y = 24$
Now subtract the new second equation from the original first equation.
$3x + 3y = 15$
$\underline{-(3x + 6y = 24)}$
$-3y = -9$
Then solve for y.
$-3y = -9$
$-3y \div -3 = -9 \div -3$
$y = 3$
Using our original second equation of $x + 2y = 8$, substitute the value of 3 for y to solve for x.
$x + 2y = 8$
$x + (2 \times 3) = 8$
$x + 6 = 8$
$x + 6 - 6 = 8 - 6$
$x = 2$

99) The correct answer is B. There is a difference of 4 between each number in the sequence.
Where variable a represents your starting number and variable d represents the difference, you could write an arithmetic sequence like this: a, a + d, a + 2d, a + 3d, a + 4d, a + 5d, . . .

However, it is easier to remember that the formula for the nth number of an arithmetic sequence is: $a + [d \times (n - 1)]$ We can prove that 21 is the sixth number of the sequence in our problem by putting the values into the formula.

$a = 1$

$d = 4$

$n = 6$

$a + [d \times (n - 1)]$

$1 + [4 \times (6 - 1)] =$

$1 + (4 \times 5) =$

$1 + 20 = 21$

100) The correct answer is D. Each number in the sequence is found by multiplying by a factor of 3:

$2 \times 3 = 6$

$6 \times 3 = 18$

$18 \times 3 = 54$

So, each subsequent number is found by multiplying the previous number by 3. Where the first number is represented by variable a and the factor (called the "common ratio") is represented by variable r, you could write out a geometric sequence like this: $a, ar, a(r)^2, a(r)^3 \ldots$

The sequence in this problem starts at 2 and triples each time, so $a = 2$ (the first term) and $r = 3$ (the "common ratio"). Remember that the formula for calculating the nth item in a geometric sequence is as follows: $ar^{(n-1)}$

So, let's consider our example problem again.

2, 6, 18, 54, . . .

The fifth term of the sequence is $54 \times 3 = 162$.

We can check this by putting the values into our formula: $ar^{(n-1)}$

$a = 2$ (the first term)

$r = 3$ (the "common ratio")

$n = 5$

$2 \times 3^{(5 - 1)} =$

$2 \times 3^4 =$

$2 \times 81 = 162$

Made in United States
Orlando, FL
06 February 2023

29617070R00104